What Happens One Second After We Die?
(Volume 2 of 5)

In the first volume of our series we considered what the Bible had to say about living in the light of eternity. We began by covering the subjects of death, dying, and the afterlife. We found that death is not the end. Indeed, it leads to an ultimate destination. For believers, it is in the presence of the Lord but for unbelievers it consists of eternal separation from Him. Understanding these biblical truths will help us live our lives in the light of the eternity which awaits us.

In this book, we will look at what the Bible has to say about the state of those who have died. What happens to people "one second" after they die? Are they conscious, or do they sleep? Do believers go immediately to heaven and unbelievers immediately to hell? What does the Bible say?

We will consider these and other related questions as we examine this important topic of the present state of the dead.

Does A Temporary State For The Dead Actually Exist?

As we examine the Scriptures, we discover that human beings will exist in three different stages, or phases.

First, it is our time here upon the earth. After our death, we will all enter into a transitional state between this life and our final destination. It is variously termed the intermediate state or the in-between state. This state of existence is only temporary.

There will eventually be a resurrection of our dead bodies and then a judgment. Once this takes place, we will enter into the third and final stage of our existence, eternity.

This is what the Scripture teaches on the subject. However, there are some Bible-believers who reject the idea of an in-between state. They insist that the dead go to their ultimate or eternal destination immediately upon death, either heaven or hell. In other words, there is no temporary state, no waiting period.

They offer a number of objections to the idea of an in-between state between this life and our eternal destination. Therefore, before we look at what the Bible has to say about an in-between state for the dead, we must demonstrate that it actually exists. We will do so by listing their main objections and then giving a biblical response to each of them.

OBJECTION 1: THE INTERMEDIATE STATE TAKES AWAY FROM GOD'S PROMISES

It is sometimes objected that the idea of a temporary state diminishes the promises of God for the believer. Instead of receiving all that God has promised to us upon our death, the Christian is merely waiting for these promises to occur. For those who believed in Jesus Christ during the New Testament times, this waiting has already taken two thousand years.

RESPONSE

The promises of God are not in any way diminished if there is an interval of time between now and their ultimate fulfillment. In fact, many promises in Scripture will not be completely fulfilled until Jesus Christ returns.

Furthermore, those who have trusted Jesus are in a place of complete joy and happiness. Indeed, they are in the presence of the Lord! In other words, they are lacking nothing.

OBJECTION 2: WE SHOULD NOT ASSUME THERE IS TIME IN THE AFTERLIFE

Another objection to an intermediate state involves time. It is asked why we should assume that time is the same for those who are dead as it is for the living. Is it not possible that those who have died will immediately wake up upon death to all of the promises that God has for them? This being the case, we should not assume there is such thing as an intermediate or in-between state.

RESPONSE

While it is true that things in the eternal state will not operate in the same way as they do here upon the earth, this does not necessarily mean that time will be done away with.

Indeed, there are passages in the New Testament which seem to indicate that those in heaven are viewing the events upon the earth in the exact same sequence, or time, in which they are occurring.

For example, we are told in the Book of Revelation that the martyrs in heaven are waiting to be vindicated.

> Now when the Lamb opened the fifth seal, I saw under the altar the souls of those who had been violently killed because of the word of God and because of the testimony they had given. They cried out with a loud voice, "How long, Sovereign Master, holy and true, before you judge those who live on the earth and avenge our blood" (Revelation 6:9,10 NET).

From these verses, it seems that these dead believers in heaven are, in some sense, bound by our time frame. In other words, they are waiting for events upon the earth to unfold. If this is the case, then this objection to the idea of a temporary state of the dead does not have much weight.

OBJECTION 3: IT TAKES AWAY FROM THE WORTH OF THE HUMAN BODY IF PEOPLE LIVE BODILESS

Many people believe that in the intermediate state the believer lives consciously without a body. It is argued that this takes away from the worth that the Bible ascribes to our bodies. In other words, it lessens the meaning of our human form if we can exist hundreds or thousands of years in a bodiless state.

RESPONSE

There are several ways to respond to this objection. For one thing, this assumes that a bodiless state is inferior to the state of having a body. If that were the case, then God would be an inferior being to us! Scripture says that God is spirit; He does not have a body. Jesus said.

> God is spirit, and his worshipers must worship in the Spirit and in truth (John 4:24 NIV).

Furthermore, angels do not have bodies either. From the writer to the Hebrews we are told that they are ministering spirits.

Are they not all ministering spirits sent out to serve for the sake of those who are to inherit salvation (Hebrews 1:14 ESV).

Are we to assume that God created them as inferior beings because they do not have any physical form? Actually, Scripture teaches just the opposite.

What is man that you think of him or the son of man that you care for him? You made him lower than the angels for a little while (Hebrews 2:7,8 NET).

These verses tell us that humans were made "lower" than the angels. In other words, these bodiless beings are a superior type of being to us; at least for the present time.

So the idea that we may be bodiless for a period of time after our death does not take away from our worth as human beings.

However, it is by no means certain that the intermediate state is a bodiless state. Indeed, many people think that the Scripture teaches that believers will have some sort of temporary body immediately upon their death. We will deal with this question later in the book.

OBJECTION 4: SCRIPTURE EMPHASIZES THE BLESSINGS GIVEN TO THE ENTIRE COMMUNITY OF BELIEVERS, NOT JUST INDIVIDUALS

When the Bible emphasizes the future promises of God for those who have believed, it is always in the context of blessing *all* believers. An intermediate or temporary state does not accomplish this. In fact, only some individual believers are blessed because the body of Christ, the church, is incomplete. The living believers have certainly not entered the world of the afterlife. In addition, those who have died are still waiting for the fulfillment of all the promises which God made to them.

Furthermore, there are still an unknown number of people who have not yet been born who will eventually be in God's presence. Therefore, an intermediate state cannot be one of blessedness for all believers since all believers have not passed on from this life.

RESPONSE

It is true that the promises given to believers consists of promises given to the entire church, the body of Christ. However, this does not mean that all Christians will benefit from these promises at the same time. Indeed, the entire community of believers is still in the process of being formed. This being the case, we should not exclude the possibility of God blessing the deceased believers while waiting to complete His promises to those who have not yet died.

THE OBJECTIONS TO AN INTERMEDIATE STATE ARE NOT CONVINCING

The various objections to the idea of an intermediate or temporary state of the dead have reasonable answers. Indeed, as we will discover, there are so many passages which we find in the Bible that seem to necessitate an in-between state for the dead before all of the promises of God are fully realized by the believer.

This being the case, we conclude that all believers in Jesus Christ who have died will spend time in this in-between state before receiving everything which God has promised them for their eternal future.

SUMMARY TO QUESTION 1
DOES A TEMPORARY STATE FOR THE DEAD ACTUALLY EXIST?

The intermediate, or in-between, state is the time between the death of a person and the fulfillment of all of the promises of God recorded in Scripture. In other words, it is only a temporary state of existence.

According to the Bible, our lives are, therefore, in three stages. First, is our existence here upon the earth. Once we die we enter a temporary state of existence while we wait for our final destination. This state will end when the dead are raised and judged. At that time, the believers will be eternally in the presence of the Lord while unbelievers will be eternally separated from Him and all His blessings.

Yet, not every Bible-believer is convinced that such a temporary state truly exists. For a number of reasons, they reject the idea of an in-between state. As we discovered, their objections are not convincing.

For one thing, it is objected that an intermediate state delays God's promises to the believer. Instead of receiving these promises upon death the believer must wait until the return of Jesus Christ for the fulfillment. In some cases, people have already been waiting for about two thousand years.

However, this objection is really without merit. Many of the promises of God have taken time to come to pass. For example, Israel waited hundreds of years in slavery before their deliverance to the Promised Land. They also waited thousands of years before Jesus the Messiah arrived on the scene. Waiting certainly does not diminish the promises of God. This is especially true if deceased believers are waiting in a state of complete bliss and comfort.

It is also contended that we should not assume that time is the same for those who have died. Some argue that as soon as believers die they immediately experience all which God has promised because they are not limited by time constraints in eternity. Therefore, there is no "incomplete state" for believers.

This objection is not convincing. Why should we assume that those in the next world are not bound by some sort of time constraints? This objection would seemingly say that for those who have died Jesus is now reigning in the New Jerusalem, the old heaven and earth have passed away, and the final judgment has occurred. But none of these things have happened.

In addition, we saw that the martyrs in the Book of Revelation were crying out to the Lord to be avenged. In fact, they specifically asked Him how long they would have to wait for this to take place. Consequently, those in the next world seem to be bound by some sort of time.

A third objection deals with the human body. If believers live in a bodiless state while waiting for their resurrection body does this not take away from the meaning of our body?

Again, this objection is not that difficult to deal with. For one thing, we do not know if the believers in the afterlife are bodiless. There may be some type of temporary body that fits the world in which they are in. We do not have enough information to be certain.

Furthermore, God Himself as well as the angelic realm are bodiless. In other words, they exist without the same type of physical shell that each of us have. They are in no way diminished as genuine personages because they do not have a physical body. Indeed, nobody wants to say that God is somehow inferior to us since He does not have a body! Thus, this objection does not stand.

Finally, there is the observation that all the promises of God are given in a context of the entire community of believers. A temporary state involves only those believers who have died to this point. Therefore, the in-between state diminishes what God has promised to all the saints because it emphasizes individual blessings and not corporate blessings.

We can respond to this by noting that the promises will indeed come to pass for the entire community of believers but that group has not yet been formed. This, however, does not mean that those who have passed on should have to wait for God's blessings until they are joined by all believers. Certainly, those in a temporary state can enjoy the presence of the Lord while waiting for the complete fulfillment of His promises. Nothing precludes the individual deceased believers receiving God's blessings while waiting for other believers to join them.

Therefore, while objections can be made against the idea of an in-between or temporary state for the dead, these objections are not convincing. There is too much evidence in Scripture of a time when the dead are consciously waiting for the fulfillment of all God's promises. While these believers are in this temporary period they are being comforted and blessed by God Himself.

QUESTION 2

According To The Old Testament What Happened To People Immediately Upon Death (Sheol)

The Bible says that we humans have both a physical and a spiritual nature. When a person dies the spiritual nature, the spirit, and the physical nature, the body, separate. The lifeless body goes to the grave but the spirit goes somewhere else. This is the main idea behind the word death in the Bible; it involves a separation, a separation of the body and the spirit.

While the body cannot live without the spirit, the opposite is not the case. Indeed, the spirit can live without the body. In fact, the Bible says that our spirit lives on forever because each of us has been made for eternity.

Consequently, while death brings an end to what we do in this life, it is certainly not the end of us. Death brings all of us to another destination. We only know these truths because God has revealed them to us in the Bible. Therefore, to receive answers to our questions on the afterlife we must study what the Scripture has to say.

SHEOL, THE PLACE OF THE DEAD

In the Old Testament, we are told that the dead go to a place called "Sheol." Generally speaking, this Hebrew word refers to the grave, the physical place where those who have died are buried. Therefore, the righteous, as well as the unrighteous, all go to Sheol. This is the primary meaning of the word.

In other contexts, Sheol refers to deep in the earth's surface. In each of these instances, it has the physical world in mind.

Some people see it as its *only* meaning. In other words, it simply means the grave or the surface underneath the earth, nothing else.

However, others see the word referring also to the unseen realm of the dead, the netherworld, the underworld. It is the place where the spirits of those who have passed on are now living. While the term originally meant the grave, it eventually came to refer to the place of the departed spirits of the unrighteous dead.

THERE ARE PASSAGES THAT MAY INDICATE THE SPIRITS OF THE DEAD GATHER TOGETHER

While most of the references to Sheol speak of the actual grave, the physical earth beneath us, there are a few Old Testament passages that refer to the spirits of the dead being gathered together in the unseen realm. Thus, in Sheol, they live a conscious existence. We read about this in the writings of the prophet Isaiah.

> Sheol beneath is stirred up to meet you when you come; it rouses the shades to greet you, all who were leaders of the earth; it raises from their thrones all who were kings of the nations. All of them will answer and say to you: 'You too have become as weak as we! You have become like us!' Your pomp is brought down to Sheol, the sound of your harps; maggots are laid as a bed beneath you, and worms are your covers (Isaiah 14:9-11 ESV).

This passage speaks of Sheol as a place where the spirits of the dead congregate.

If this passage is to be understood literally, then Sheol can refer to more than the mere place of burial or somewhere deep in the physical earth.

However, some see this as a poetic passage. Consequently, they argue that these verses are not to be interpreted as speaking of an actual place where spirits live.

THE SHADES WHO LIVE IN SHEOL

The Old Testament also speaks of shadowy figures who exist in the netherworld known as the "shades." We read about them in Proverbs.

> For her way leads down to death, and her paths to the shades (Proverbs 2:18 NRSV).

Some English versions translate the word as "departed spirits."

> For her house sinks down to death and her ways to the land of the departed spirits (Proverbs 2:18 HCSB).

Again, if we understand this literally, then the Old Testament did speak of the spirits of the dead still existing in the underworld (for more on the shades see Appendix 3).

While there is debate as to whether these particular references are to be understood literally, the Old Testament clearly teaches that death is not the end of our existence.

TALKING TO THE DEAD IS FORBIDDEN

Indeed, the Old Testament forbids, in the strongest of terms, the living contacting the dead. For example, we read the following warnings.

> There shall not be found among you anyone who burns his son or his daughter as an offering, anyone who practices divination or tells fortunes or interprets omens, or a sorcerer or a charmer or a medium or a necromancer or one who inquires of the dead (Deuteronomy 18:10-11 ESV).

19

In this verse, the Lord warned Israel about attempting to talk to the dead.

In the Book of Isaiah, we discover further warnings about the living contacting the dead.

> And when they say to you, "Inquire of the mediums and the necromancers who chirp and mutter," should not a people inquire of their God? Should they inquire of the dead on behalf of the living (Isaiah 8:19 ESV).

If the dead ceased to exist, then there would be no reason whatsoever for these prohibitions. Indeed, these commandments assume that the dead still consciously exist somewhere in the unseen realm. Otherwise there would be no need to give these warnings about attempting to contact them.

THE DEAD PROPHET SAMUEL APPEARED SAUL AT EN DOR

We also have the account of Saul contacting the dead prophet Samuel at the city of En Dor (1 Samuel 28). The fact that Samuel appeared shows that the dead do not go out of existence (We examine this episode in detail in Question 14).

DAVID SAID HE WOULD GO TO BE WITH HIS DECEASED SON

There is also the story of King David and his infant son who was dying. When David heard of his death, he stopped fasting and praying. He washed himself, ordered food, and worshipped the Lord. Those around him were surprised by his actions. The Bible records his response.

> But now he is dead. Why should I fast? Can I bring him back again? I shall go to him, but he will not return to me (2 Samuel 12:23 ESV).

When David said, "I shall go to him," he was not merely saying that he would join his child in death. Certainly there would not be much comfort in that! David had a belief in something more. There is life after this life where he would see his son again.

This is further confirmed by the fact that David did not mourn for his son after he died. He knew that they would re-unite some day. We also read.

> Then David comforted Bathsheba, his wife (2 Samuel 12:24).

What comfort could he give Bathsheba? It was the comfort of knowing that she too would see her son again.

There is something else we can add to this. In the New Testament, we are told the following about King David.

> He was a prophet (Acts 2:30 NLT).

A prophet is someone who speaks for God. On the occasion of the death of his infant son, it seems that David spoke prophetically of his destiny; he would see his infant son again. Not merely in death, but in a conscious afterlife. Knowing this truth gave the king both comfort and assurance.

THE DEAD WILL BE RAISED

Consequently, while the meaning of Sheol may be debated, what is not debatable is that the Old Testament looked forward to the time when the dead would be raised. We read the following in the Book of Daniel.

> At that time Michael, the great prince who protects your people, will arise. There will be a time of distress such as has not happened from the beginning of nations until then. But at that time your people—everyone whose name is found written in the book—will be delivered. Multitudes who sleep in the dust of the earth will awake: some to everlasting life, others to shame and everlasting contempt (Daniel 12:1,2 NIV).

In this passage we have the promise of a future resurrection and judgment of both believers and unbelievers. All of humanity will ultimately be resurrected and judged.

We conclude that the Old Testament has little to say on the matter of a temporary or in-between state of the dead. As we will see, this is not the same with the New Testament. Indeed, it gives us quite a bit of information about what happens to a person the moment they die. Thus, our study will concentrate on what the New Testament says.

SUMMARY TO QUESTION 2
ACCORDING TO THE OLD TESTAMENT, WHAT HAPPENED TO PEOPLE IMMEDIATELY UPON DEATH (SHEOL)

The Hebrew word Sheol is mainly used to refer to the place where the dead are buried, the grave, or in some instances, the ground beneath us. It may also refer to the place where the spirits of the dead reside, the netherworld. However, this is not certain.

There are also a few passages that refer to the "shades" of Sheol. Some versions translate this as the "departed spirits of the dead." If these references are to be understood literally and not figuratively, then we have specific references to those spirits living in the underworld.

As we search the Old Testament we find that there is not much information about the intermediate, the in-between state of the dead. Yet we do know that it was assumed that the dead continued to exist.

First, we have the warnings in the Old Testament about the living attempting to contact the dead. This would make no sense whatsoever if it was assumed that the deceased merely went out of existence. Forbidding the living to contact the dead indicates the belief that it was possible to do this. Moreover, we have the account of the dead prophet Samuel appearing to King Saul at the city of En Dor.

In addition, we have the response of King David when his infant son died. David stopped praying and fasting, he asked for something to eat and then worshipped the Lord. When asked about his behavior David said that his son would not come back to him but rather he would join that "little one" some day.

It certainly seems that David was thinking about more than joining him in death. Rather David had a belief that he would join him in the afterlife. Since David was a prophet, it is sensible to assume that he was speaking prophetically here of his future. Indeed, he was comforted with the fact that he would see his son again.

Finally, the Old Testament looked forward to a day when the dead would be raised and judged. The last chapter of the Book of Daniel makes this clear. Consequently, death was not seen as the end of all existence for humans.

What we do know is that the New Testament provides us with much more information on what happens immediately to humans upon their death. Therefore, our study of the in-between state will concentrate on what the New Testament teaches on this subject.

According To The New Testament What Happens To The Dead? (Hades)

In the Old Testament the dead went to a place called Sheol. When speaking of the dead, it is possible that it is only referring to the actual place where the dead are buried, the grave. However, others argue that it also has reference to the place where the departed spirits gather in the unseen realm, a place where they are conscious.

As is true with many biblical teachings, the information we have about the in-between state was sketchy in Old Testament times. It was not until the time of Jesus Christ that conditions in the realm of the dead were more fully revealed.

JESUS REVEALED DETAILED INFORMATION ABOUT THE AFTERLIFE

In the four gospels, we find that Jesus provides us with further revelation on the afterlife. Among other things, He told us about a place where the dead reside. It is called in Greek, "Hades."

Therefore, it is important that we learn what we can about this place Hades; the place where the dead go according to the New Testament.

THE DEFINITION OF HADES

The word Hades has a number of different meanings in the New Testament. They include the following.

1. THE GRAVE—THE PLACE OF BODILY DECAY

2. THE PLACE OF PUNISHMENT FOR THE WICKED

3. POSSIBLY AS A GENERAL TERM FOR THE UNSEEN REALM OF THE DEAD

Generally speaking, these are the three ways in which the term is used in the New Testament.

SOME INITIAL OBSERVATIONS ABOUT HADES

There are a number of things about Hades that we must learn at the outset.

For one thing, Hades is always connected with death, never with life. Indeed, the dead are in Hades, not people living on the earth.

While it does speak of the dead, it does not refer specifically, or exclusively, to a place of punishment. In other words, it is an intermediate place for all of the dead.

In addition, it never refers to the place of final punishment of the wicked. In fact, we will discover that Hades will one day cease to exist.

Consequently, since the word can mean a number of different things, the context will always determine its meaning.

THE NEW TESTAMENT AND HADES

The New Testament says the following about Hades.

1. HADES IS THE GRAVE—THE PLACE OF BODILY DECAY

Hades can refer to the actual place where the dead are buried, the place of bodily decay, the grave.

On the Day of Pentecost, Peter said the following about the death of Jesus.

Dear brothers, think about this! You can be sure that the patriarch David wasn't referring to himself, for he died and was buried, and his tomb is still here among us. But he was a prophet, and he knew God had promised with an oath that one of David's own descendants would sit on his throne. David was looking into the future and speaking of the Messiah's resurrection. He was saying that God would not leave him among the dead or allow his body to rot in the grave (Acts 2:29-31 NLT).

In this context, Hades is an obvious reference to the grave, the place of burial. Peter said that the prophecy which David made could not have been about himself since his body did decay, it did decompose in the grave. Indeed, his tomb was still there in the city of Jerusalem.

However, the grave would have no victory over the Messiah. His body would not lie in decay in Hades, the grave. Jesus came back from the dead. Unlike David, His body did not remain in the grave. Thus, in this context, Hades has a simple meaning, the grave.

2. HADES IS THE PLACE OF TEMPORARY PUNISHMENT FOR THE WICKED

Hades is also used to refer to a place of temporary punishment of the unrighteous dead. Jesus told the story of the rich man and Lazarus. Luke records Him giving the following story.

And in Hades, being in torment, he lifted up his eyes and saw Abraham far off and Lazarus at his side. And he called out, 'Father Abraham, have mercy on me, and send Lazarus to dip the end of his finger in water and cool my tongue, for I am in anguish in this flame.' But Abraham said, 'Child, remember that you in your lifetime received your good things, and Lazarus in like manner bad things; but now he is comforted here, and you are in anguish. And besides all this, between us and you a great chasm has been fixed, in order

that those who would pass from here to you may not be able,
and none may cross from there to us (Luke 16:23-26 ESV).

In this context, Hades speaks of the place where the wicked go after their lives are over. It is a place of punishment. It is an intermediate state, an in-between state. It is somewhere between this life and their ultimate destination which is hell, the lake of fire. In this story, the rich man was sent to Hades, this temporary place of punishment.

In another instance in the gospels, we find Jesus using Hades as a term referring to the punishment of the wicked. He had some strong words of condemnation to say to certain cities that saw His miracles, but did not accept Him as the promised Messiah. The Lord said that they would be brought down to Hades. We find Him saying the following about the city where He made His headquarters, Capernaum.

> And you, Capernaum, will you be lifted to the heavens? No, you will go down to Hades. For if the miracles that were performed in you had been performed in Sodom, it would have remained to this day (Matthew 11:23 NIV).

These wicked people in Capernaum would eventually be punished in Hades because of their willful rejection of Jesus as the Messiah. They were singled out for special punishment because of the biblical principle "to whom much is given much is expected." Therefore, we have another passage which equates Hades with punishment.

3. HADES MAY HAVE BEEN THE PLACE FOR THE RIGHTEOUS DEAD

In the account we just referred to in Luke 16, there is some question as to whether Lazarus and Abraham were in Hades or in heaven. If they were in Hades, they were in a place that was separated from the unrighteous dead. What we do discover is that the unseen realm is divided between the saved and the lost. They do not all live together in the same place in the afterlife.

HADES IS DISTINGUISHED FROM DEATH

There are some other observations which we can make about Hades. In the Book of Revelation, it is distinguished from death itself. We read the following description of one of the four horses of the apocalypse.

> I looked and there was a pale green horse! Its rider's name was Death, and Hades followed with him; they were given authority over a fourth of the earth, to kill with sword, famine, and pestilence, and by the wild animals of the earth (Revelation 6:8 NRSV).

In this context, Hades is not the same as death but is closely linked to it.

HADES WILL BE DESTROYED ONE DAY

In addition, we discover that Hades is not a permanent place. Indeed, it is only temporary. It will cease to exist at some future time. We read the following in the Book of Revelation about what will happen to Hades.

> The sea gave up the dead that were in it, and death and Hades gave up the dead that were in them, and each person was judged according to what he had done. Then death and Hades were thrown into the lake of fire. The lake of fire is the second death (Revelation 20:13,14 NIV).

Because Hades will someday be destroyed, it is not to be seen as the ultimate abode of the unbelieving dead. There is a destination beyond it, hell, the lake of fire.

JESUS HAS THE KEY TO HADES

Jesus Himself has the keys to death and Hades. We read of this in the Book of Revelation. John wrote.

> I am He who lives, and was dead, and behold, I am alive forevermore. Amen. And I have the keys of Hades and of Death (Revelation 1:18 NKJV).

The Bible emphasizes that Jesus Christ has conquered death and the grave. Therefore, He has complete authority over them. This is one of the great truths of Scripture!

ONLY THE UNBELIEVING DEAD GO THERE NOW

Hades, in the sense of referring to the place of departed spirits, is now a place for only the unbelieving dead. We are told that the righteous go to be with the Lord when they die, Paul wrote.

> Yes, we are of good courage, and we would rather be away from the body and at home with the Lord (2 Corinthians 5:8 ESV).

Believers go immediately to be with the Lord upon their death. As soon as a Christian takes his or her last breath in this world they are in the presence of Jesus Christ in the next world.

Therefore, from a study of the totality of the New Testament we discover a number of different truths about the intermediate state of the dead, Hades.

As we have observed, since the word has a number of meanings and shades of meaning, we always have to study the context to determine exactly what it meant.

SUMMARY TO QUESTION 3
ACCORDING TO THE NEW TESTAMENT WHAT HAPPENS TO THE DEAD? (HADES)

We have discovered that the Old Testament does not have much to say about the subject of the intermediate or in-between state of the dead. In fact, the Hebrew word Sheol, which is used of the dead, may only refer to the physical place where they are buried, the grave.

However, the New Testament gives us much more information on the subject with the Greek word "Hades." It refers to a number of different things.

Sometimes Hades refers simply to the grave, the place where the dead presently reside. Those who have died are now in Hades, or in the grave.

Yet it also refers to the specific place where the wicked suffer after death. In Jesus' story of the rich man and Lazarus, the rich man was suffering in Hades while Lazarus was not. In this context, the word has a more specific meaning.

It has been argued Hades may also be a general term for the unseen realm of the dead, but this is not clear. What we do know is that Hades is never used of the final destination of anyone, righteous or unrighteous. It is only a temporary place.

Scripture says that Jesus Christ has the key to death and Hades. His victory over death, as well as the grave, means that someday these two terrors will no longer exist. Indeed, Hades along with death will end someday.

The Book of Revelation informs us that death and Hades will be thrown into the lake of fire at the Last Judgment. Never again will they terrorize humans, for death and Hades will not exist in the eternal realm of God.

Indeed, the Lord will create an entire new heaven and new earth where all the previous things will have passed away. This includes all things which are evil. They will be no more. This is the wonderful promise of Scripture.

Finally, since believers go immediately to be with the Lord upon their death, Hades now only holds the spirits of the unbelieving dead.

In sum, because the world Hades is used in a number of ways, it is vital that we always interpret it in the context in which we find it.

QUESTION 4

In The Old Testament Era, Was The Unseen Realm Of The Dead Divided Into Two Compartments?

In the Gospel according to Luke, Jesus told a story of two people who died about the same time but went to two very different places. A rich man died and went to Hades where he was in torment. A poor man named Lazarus died but he went to a place of happiness and bliss called "Abraham's bosom" or "Abraham's side."

From the account that Jesus told of the rich man and Lazarus, some have seen a division that existed in Hades, the unseen realm of the dead. They believe that Hades was divided into two compartments in Jesus' day; the abode of the righteous and the abode of the unrighteous.

Is this what the Bible teaches on the subject?

THE TWO COMPARTMENTS THEORY: HADES HAD TWO PARTS

This theory can be summed up as follows: In the unseen realm of the dead Hades was made up of two compartments; an upper and a lower. The upper level was called Abraham's bosom, or Abraham's side, while the lower level was the place of torments. The righteous dead were in the upper level, while the unrighteous dead exist in the lower. This makes it possible for the ones in the lower level to look up at the ones in the upper.

However, those in the lower level could not ascend to the upper level and those in the upper level could not come down to the lower level. This division into these two compartments existed only before the ascension of Christ. After that, there was no such division. The following points are usually made in support of the theory.

1. SHEOL AND HADES ARE THE SAME PLACE

This view identifies Sheol with Hades in the realm of the dead, the netherworld. According to the Old Testament, both the righteous and unrighteous went down to Sheol. Consequently, it is argued, there must have been two compartments of the unseen realm of the dead until the time of Christ; one for the righteous and the other for the unrighteous.

2. BEFORE THE TIME OF JESUS CHRIST THERE WAS NO ADMITTANCE TO HEAVEN

It is also contended that before Jesus Christ came and died for the sins of the world, there was no admittance to heaven for believers. Their sins were not taken away or forgiven, but merely atoned for, or covered up, until He died on the cross of Calvary. In fact the writer to the Hebrews emphasized this.

> In fact, the law requires that nearly everything be cleansed with blood, and without the shedding of blood there is no forgiveness (Hebrews 9:22 NIV).

Therefore, heaven could not be accessed by humans until Christ had taken away our sin by dying as our substitute.

3. THE BARRIER HAS BEEN REMOVED

The barrier between God and humanity was removed by Christ's sacrifice of Himself on the cross. The Bible says.

Nor was it to offer himself repeatedly, as the high priest enters the holy places every year with blood not his own for then he would have had to suffer repeatedly since the foundation of the world. But as it is, he has appeared once for all at the end of the ages to put away sin by the sacrifice of himself (Hebrews 9:25,26 ESV).

The Contemporary English Version puts it this way

If he had offered himself every year, he would have suffered many times since the creation of the world. But instead, near the end of time he offered himself once and for all, so that he could be a sacrifice that does away with sin (Hebrews 9:26 CEV).

When Christ came and once-and-for-all died for the sins of the world, the way was made for believers to enter heaven. Access is now available to all because of His death.

4. JESUS BROUGHT THE RIGHTEOUS OUT OF SHEOL

Upon His ascension, Jesus emptied the righteous people out of Sheol, or Hades, and brought them into the presence of God the Father. Paul wrote about this in his letter to the Ephesians. He explained what Christ did upon His ascension.

Therefore it is said, "When he ascended on high he made captivity itself a captive; he gave gifts to his people." (When it says, "He ascended," what does it mean but that he had also descended into the lower parts of the earth? He who descended is the same one who ascended far above all the heavens, so that he might fill all things.) (Ephesians 4:8-10 NRSV).

To retrieve the righteous dead, the text says he descended into the lower parts of the earth. This would be the location of Sheol/Hades. Since the ascension of Jesus, the righteous dead are in now the presence of the Lord, while the unrighteous dead remain in the place of torments in Hades.

There are some people that see a statement of Jesus in the Book of Revelation as referring to bringing the righteous dead to heaven.

> I *am* He who lives, and was dead, and behold, I am alive forevermore. Amen. And I have the keys of Hades and of Death (Revelation 1:18 NKJV).

They believe Christ unlocked the part of Hades that contained the righteous dead and then brought them to heaven.

5. ALL BELIEVERS NOW GO DIRECTLY TO HEAVEN

About twenty years after Jesus' ascension, Paul wrote of his experience to the Corinthians.

> I know a man in Christ who was caught up into the third heaven 14 years ago. Whether he was in the body or out of the body, I don't know; God knows. I know that this man—whether in the body or out of the body I do not know, God knows—was caught up into paradise. He heard inexpressible words, which a man is not allowed to speak (2 Corinthians 12:2-4 HCSB).

When Paul went into the presence of the Lord, he went up, not down. Therefore, it is contended that this is evidence that Jesus moved people from Hades, which is referred to as being down, to heaven which is always spoken of as being upward.

Previously the believers were geographically down. For example, when the medium at En Dor saw the dead prophet Samuel she explained it in this manner.

> The king said to her, "Don't be afraid. What do you see?" The woman said, "I see a ghostly figure coming up out of the earth." "What does he look like?" he asked. "An old man wearing a robe is coming up," she said. Then

Saul knew it was Samuel, and he bowed down and pros-
trated himself with his face to the ground. Samuel said
to Saul, "Why have you disturbed me by bringing me up
(1 Samuel 28:13-15 NIV).

Note that he came up "out of the earth." Since Samuel was among
the righteous dead, it is argued that they too were located somewhere
beneath, not somewhere above. Their location changed when Christ
came back from the dead.

This briefly sums up the two compartment theory. There are many
people who believe this is the best way in which to understand the
evidence.

OBJECTIONS TO THE TWO COMPARTMENT THEORY

Not all Bible students agree with this. Indeed, it seems that the two
compartment theory has some insurmountable difficulties. We can list
them as follows.

1. EPHESIANS 4 DOES NOT REFER TO CHRIST LEADING THE DEAD FROM HADES

To begin with, a number of Bible commentators believe that Ephesians
4:8 does not refer to Christ leading the captives from Sheol or Hades
into heaven at His ascension. They argue for one of two options.

Option one sees this passage as referring to Jesus, God the Son, coming
to the earth when He became a human being. It has no reference to
Him going into Hades, or the lower part of the earth.

In fact, we find that a number of Bible translations understand the passage in this way. The New English Translation reads.

Therefore it says, " When he ascended on high he captured
captives; he gave gifts to men." Now what is the meaning of

⌐ "he ascended," except that he also descended to the lower regions, namely, the earth? (Ephesians 4:8,9 NET).

We find something similar in the English Standard Version.

In saying, "He ascended," what does it mean but that he had also descended into the lower regions, the earth? (Ephesians 4:9 ESV).

The New Living Translation likewise translates it in the same way.

Notice that it says "he ascended." This clearly means that Christ also descended to our lowly world (Ephesians 4:9 NLT).

We also read the following from the New English Bible.

Now the word 'ascended' implies that he also descended to the lowest level, down to the very earth (Ephesians 4:9 The New English Bible).

These translations all understand that the "lower regions" or the "lowest level" is merely another way of saying, "the earth." In this verse, the earth is in contrast to heaven from where Jesus originated. Before He ascended into heaven He had to first come to the earth. Therefore, it is speaking of His First Coming to the earth and the events surrounding it.

The second option also sees the lower parts as referring to the earth itself. However, the descent in the passage does not refer to Christ coming to the earth. It is argued that the descent occurs *after* the ascent to earth by Christ, rather than before it. Consequently, it refers to the descent of the Holy Spirit at Pentecost. At that time, the risen Christ gave gifts to people.

If either of these latter two options is the correct meaning of the verse, then it has nothing to do with Jesus bringing the dead believers into the presence of the Lord from underneath the earth at the time of His ascension.

WHAT DOES IT MEAN THAT HE CAPTURED CAPTIVES?

There is another problem with seeing this as emptying out a compartment in the unseen realm of the dead. In Ephesians 4:8, Paul said Jesus "captured captives." He is loosely citing Psalm 68:18 as a prophecy of the Messiah. The psalm says that He would ascend to heaven, would conquer His enemies and lead "them" captive. The captives, therefore, are not believers but rather His foes.

In sum, while the lower parts of the earth have sometimes been taken to refer to Hades, or the unseen realm of the dead, it would not fit in with the argument here. Indeed, Jesus' ascension necessitated a previous descent to the earth but not to Hades or the netherworld.

We could also add that the Scriptures indicate that Christ's spirit went to heaven, not Hades, when He died.

> And he said to him, "Truly, I say to you, today you will be with me in Paradise ... Then Jesus, calling out with a loud voice, said, "Father, into your hands I commit my spirit!" And having said this he breathed his last (Luke 23:43, 46 ESV).

In sum, at His ascension, the Lord gave certain gifts to believers so that they could do the work of the Christian ministry. The emphasis is upon gifts given by Jesus to those who are living as the following verses in Ephesians 4 make clear.

> So Christ himself gave the apostles, the prophets, the evangelists, the pastors and teachers, to equip his people for works of service, so that the body of Christ may be built up (Ephesians 4:11,12 NIV).

Nothing in this context is speaking about the dead!

Therefore, these verses may simply speak of Jesus the Messiah coming to earth and then eventually returning to heaven, or Jesus, after He had ascended into heaven, sending the Holy Spirit to give gifts to His people.

Whichever of these two options it may be, it is clear that nothing is said about bringing deceased believers with Him at His ascension.

Therefore, this passage should not be used to teach the two compartment idea.

2. ABRAHAM'S SIDE IS HEAVEN, SEPARATE FROM HADES

Jesus described Abraham's bosom, or Abraham's side, as a separate place from Hades. Jesus taught that it was far away from Hades, not in it. In fact, we are told that Lazarus was "carried away" to Abraham's side by angels.

> The poor man died and was carried away by the angels to be
> with Abraham (Luke 16:22 NRSV).

Since angels come from heaven, the presence of the Lord, the natural assumption would be that the angels carried him away "up to heaven," not down to some place underneath the earth. Therefore, Abraham's bosom is another description of heaven.

3. PARADISE IS EQUATED WITH HEAVEN

We also find Jesus told the robber that was crucified next to Him that they would both be immediately in paradise, not in some compartment in Hades.

> Then he said, "Jesus, remember me when you come in your
> kingdom." And Jesus said to him, "I tell you the truth, today
> you will be with me in paradise" (Luke 23:42,43 NET).

Elsewhere, we learn that paradise is synonymous with heaven; the presence of the Lord. We again refer to a passage from Paul which we earlier quoted.

> I know a man in Christ who was caught up into the third
> heaven 14 years ago. Whether he was in the body or out
> of the body, I don't know; God knows. I know that this

man—whether in the body or out of the body I do not know, God knows—was caught up into paradise. He heard inexpressible words, which a man is not allowed to speak (2 Corinthians 12:2-4 HCSB).

Notice that Paul describes himself being caught up to the "third heaven" (verse 2), and then defines this place as "paradise" (verse 4) making the terms synonymous.

Putting these three passages together we may conclude the following.

First, Abraham's bosom, or Abraham's side, was different from Hades. It was a place where angels had to bring Lazarus.

Next, we learn that paradise and the third heaven are synonymous. Therefore, Abraham's bosom was a figurative way of describing paradise, the third heaven, or the presence of God.

The criminal who died next to Jesus on the cross went to the same place Paul would later visit, paradise or heaven. Consequently, before Jesus' ascension, this criminal went to heaven upon his death.

Therefore, from the very beginning, everyone who died trusting the Lord went to heaven, not some compartment in the underworld.

3. THE OLD TESTAMENT SAINTS HAD IMMEDIATE ACCESS TO THE LORD

The entrance to heaven has always been based upon the sacrifice of Jesus on the cross. However, nothing is stated in Scripture that the Old Testament believers were kept from the presence of the Lord before the first coming of Christ. They were allowed entrance to heaven by looking forward to His sacrifice; just as we are allowed entrance by looking back.

4. WHERE DID ENOCH AND ELIJAH GO?

There is another problem with the two compartment theory. If the dead were not allowed into heaven, the presence of the Lord, until the resurrection or ascension of Christ. then where did Enoch and Elijah go when the Lord took them?

According to the Old Testament, neither of them died. Enoch was first taken and then centuries later Elijah was ushered into the presence of the Lord. They certainly went somewhere! Are we to assume when Elijah was taken to heaven only God and Enoch were there to greet him?

We also read this.

> Now when the Lord was about to take Elijah up to heaven by a whirlwind, Elijah and Elisha were on their way from Gilgal ... As they continued walking and talking, a chariot of fire and horses of fire separated the two of them, and Elijah ascended in a whirlwind into heaven (2 Kings 2:1,11 NRSV).

The fact that Elijah went "up" to heaven is a further indication that Old Testament saints were not in some temporary place in the heart of the earth. Their dead bodies were in the grave, but their spirits were with the Lord in His presence, heaven.

Indeed, we find the same description of what happened earlier to the patriarch Enoch.

> By faith Enoch was taken up so that he did not see death, and he was not to be found because God took him up (Hebrews 11:5 NET).

Again, note the direction where he was taken, "up." Enoch and Elijah went to heaven as did every Old Testament believer.

5. AT THE TRANSFIGURATION MOSES AND ELIJAH WERE SEEMINGLY TAKEN UP IN A CLOUD

At the transfiguration of Jesus Christ, the Bible says that Moses and Elijah appeared with Him. God the Father also spoke to the three disciples who were also with Jesus from a bright cloud which overshadowed them.

He was still speaking when, behold, a bright cloud overshadowed them, and a voice from the cloud said, "This is my beloved Son, with whom I am well pleased; listen to him" (Matthew 17:5 ESV).

Then Moses and Elijah disappeared in the cloud. This would strongly suggest they went upward, not downward.

There is one further thing. Since we know Elijah had previously gone to heaven we should also assume that he and Moses came from the same place when they appeared on the Mount of Transfiguration.

We should also assume that they returned to the same place together. Indeed, there is no indication that Elijah came from above while Moses joined him from below.

WHAT ABOUT EN DOR?

We also need to be careful about reading too much in the story of Saul and Samuel at En Dor. Coming up from the ground would simply mean that Samuel came back from the grave where he was buried. Indeed, the account also tells us that Samuel was wearing the same clothes that Saul last saw him wearing when he came "up from the ground."

Therefore, the fact that Samuel came up from the grave, wearing the same clothes as he had on earth, was seemingly stated to establish to Saul it was truly Samuel who was speaking to him. It was not to give us any definitive answer about where the righteous dead were residing.

However, what it does tell us is that each of us do keep our individual identity in the in-between state.

CONCLUSION: ALL BELIEVERS WENT IMMEDIATELY TO HEAVEN

The best answer seems to be that all the Old Testament saints went immediately to heaven to wait for their bodily resurrection. They will receive their new bodies when Jesus Christ returns a second time. Meanwhile, they are in a state of happiness and bliss in the presence of the Lord.

AREAS OF AGREEMENT ABOUT THE INTERMEDIATE STATE

There are a couple of issues about the intermediate state in which everyone agrees. They are as follows.

1. THE INTERMEDIATE STATE IS WONDERFUL FOR BELIEVERS

All sides agree that the in-between state is a wonderful place for the believer. They are in a place of peace and rest waiting for further promised events to unfold.

2. UNBELIEVERS STILL WAIT FOR THE FINAL JUDGMENT

All agree that unbelievers will wait in Hades until the final judgment. At that time, death and Hades will be thrown into the lake of fire. The Bible says.

> The sea gave up the dead who were in it, and Death and Hades delivered up the dead who were in them. And they were judged, each one according to his works (Revelation 20:13 NKJV).

Final judgment is still yet to come.

In sum, whatever the situation may have been for the believers in the Old Testament period, we know that today all believers go immediately to the presence of the Lord upon death.

SUMMARY TO QUESTION 4
IN THE OLD TESTAMENT ERA, WAS THE UNSEEN WORLD DIVIDED INTO TWO COMPARTMENTS?

Where did the dead go before Jesus Christ came into the world? Some people believe in what is known as the "two compartment theory." This viewpoint basically teaches that Sheol or Hades was occupied by both believers and unbelievers before the coming of Jesus Christ to the earth. The spirits of the righteous and the unrighteous dead were alive in two different divisions, or compartments, in the unseen realm, the underworld.

When Jesus ascended into heaven, He emptied out the righteous part of the unseen world and brought believers into the presence of God the Father in heaven.

The reason why believers could not go immediately to God's presence was that their sins were only covered up, not taken away. The Old Testament sacrifices looked forward to the time when Christ would come and once-and-for-all take away sin. Now that Jesus has died, risen from the dead, and ascended into heaven, there is no need for a place of waiting.

Others, however, do not believe Sheol or Hades was divided into two compartments. Indeed, there are seemingly insurmountable difficulties with this theory.

It makes more sense to assume that the righteous dead went immediately to heaven, while the unrighteous dead went to Sheol or Hades. Even though Christ had not physically taken away their sin, these people were allowed in His presence in anticipation of what He was going to do.

In addition, when we compare Scripture with Scripture, we find that Abraham's side, paradise, and the third heaven are three different ways of describing the same place.

Furthermore we also have the account of two Old Testament saints, Enoch and Elijah, who did not die. They surely went somewhere when the Lord took them. In fact, the Bible makes it clear that both Enoch and Elijah went "up" to heaven."

We certainly should not assume that only God and Enoch and Elijah were in heaven before the death and resurrection of Jesus!

Therefore, it seems that a much better answer is that all the Old Testament believers went immediately into the presence of the Lord; whether upon death, or in the case of Enoch and Elijah, when the Lord took them.

In addition, even if there were compartments in Hades before the coming of Christ, they do not exist today. The unbelieving dead still go to Hades while they await final judgment but believers go immediately to the presence of the Lord while they wait for the resurrection of their bodies and their time of reward. Bible-believers agree on these points.

QUESTION 5

Today, What Happens To A Believer Immediately Upon Death?

The intermediate state for the believer is the time in which the spirit, or soul, exists between physical death and the resurrection of the body. Though the Bible does not devote a lot of space to this topic, there are some basic conclusions we can make. They include the following.

1. THE SPIRITS OF THE BELIEVING DEAD ARE WITH GOD

The spirits of departed believers are with the Lord. This Bible clearly teaches this. For example, we read in Ecclesiastes.

> The dust returns to the ground it came from, and the spirit returns to God who gave it (Ecclesiastes 12:7 NIV).

This verse may be teaching, that in the Old Testament period, those who had died with belief in the Lord were now with Him. However, this isn't the only way that this verse can be understood.

However, the writer to the Hebrews makes it plain. He wrote the following.

> You have come to the assembly of God's firstborn children, whose names are written in heaven. You have come to God himself, who is the judge of all people. And you have come to the spirits of the redeemed in heaven who have now been made perfect (Hebrews 12:23 NLT).

There are, at this moment, redeemed people in heaven. Their perfected spirits reside in the presence of the Lord while awaiting their resurrection from the dead.

Jesus also talked about believers being with Him in the next world. In His prayer to God the Father shortly before His betrayal, trial and death, He said the following.

> Father, I desire those You have given Me to be with Me where I am. Then they will see My glory, which You have given Me because You loved Me before the world's foundation (John 17:24 HCSB).

Jesus desired that those who had trusted in Him would be with Him in the afterlife. This is a further indication that the spirits of the believing dead are with the Lord.

2. BELIEVERS ARE IN IMMEDIATELY IN CHRIST'S PRESENCE AT DEATH

We also discover that, at death, the spirit of the believer immediately enters into Christ's presence. There are a number of illustrations of this in the New Testament.

A. THE CRIMINAL NEXT TO JESUS

Jesus promised the dying criminal on the cross that he would be with Him immediately after death. Luke records the following.

> And he [Jesus] said to him, "Truly, I say to you, today you will be with me in Paradise" (Luke 23:43 ESV).

This promise also applies to each of us who believe. We will immediately be with Christ in paradise upon our deaths.

B. THE TESTIMONY OF STEPHEN: JESUS IS WAITING FOR BELIEVERS

Upon his death, the martyr Stephen called upon Jesus to receive his spirit. We read of this in the Book of Acts.

But he, full of the Holy Spirit, gazed into heaven and saw the glory of God, and Jesus standing at the right hand of God. And he said, "Behold, I see the heavens opened, and the Son of Man standing at the right hand of God." But they cried out with a loud voice and stopped their ears and rushed together at him. Then they cast him out of the city and stoned him. And the witnesses laid down their garments at the feet of a young man named Saul. And as they were stoning Stephen, he called out, "Lord Jesus, receive my spirit." And falling to his knees he cried out with a loud voice, "Lord, do not hold this sin against them." And when he had said this, he fell asleep (Acts 7:55-59 ESV).

The usual picture of Jesus is that He is sitting at the right hand of God the Father. But when Stephen was about to die, Jesus stood to welcome him into God's presence. This is another indication that the believing dead go immediately to be with Christ.

C. THE TEACHING OF THE APOSTLE PAUL TO THE CORINTHIANS

The Apostle Paul also taught that believers would be in Christ's presence upon their death. He wrote the following to the Corinthians.

Now we know that if the earthly tent we live in is destroyed, we have a building from God, an eternal house in heaven, not built by human hands. Meanwhile we groan, longing to be clothed with our heavenly dwelling ... We are confident, I say, and would prefer to be away from the body and at home with the Lord (2 Corinthians 5:1,2,8 NIV).

Paul said that being "away from the body" is to be "at home with the Lord."

The New Living Translation puts it this way.

Yes, we are fully confident, and we would rather be away from these earthly bodies, for then we will be at home with the Lord (2 Corinthians 5:8 NLT).

This is a further confirmation as to what happens to the believer one second after they die. They enter the presence of the Lord.

D. HE WROTE THE SAME TRUTH TO THE PHILIPPIANS

When Paul wrote to the church at Philippi he taught them the same truth. He spoke of his desire to depart and to be with Christ. He said.

> For I am hard pressed between the two, having a desire to depart and be with Christ, *which is* far better (Philippians 1:23 NKJV).

Paul says that his death would be far better for him than remaining alive because he would be in the presence of Christ.

E. THE EXAMPLE OF LAZARUS IN JESUS' STORY

In Jesus' story of the rich man and Lazarus, when the beggar Lazarus died, the Scripture says that he was immediately ushered into the presence of the Lord.

> The poor man died and was carried by the angels to Abraham's side. The rich man also died and was buried, and in Hades, being in torment, he lifted up his eyes and saw Abraham far off and Lazarus at his side (Luke 16:22,23 ESV).

The rich man in Hades saw both Lazarus and Abraham. Each was in a better place than the existence which he found himself. They were with the Lord!

Therefore, from these five examples, it seems clear that believers go to be immediately with the Lord upon their death.

3. THE INTERMEDIATE STATE IS NOT THE PLACE OF FINAL REWARD

Though there is an in-between state for believers, it is not the place of their final reward. In other words, it is an incomplete state. Final rewards will occur after the resurrection of the dead, which is still future. Though Christians who die go to be with the Lord, this is not the time when they receive their final reward, or their resurrection body. This is something which still awaits them in the future.

4. BELIEVERS ARE CONSCIOUS AFTER DEATH

Believers, however, are in a state of awareness after their death. Jesus told the religious leaders in His day that God was the God of the living, not of the dead. He reminded them what the Lord had said to Moses at the burning bush.

> I am the God of Abraham, the God of Isaac, and the God of Jacob? He is God not of the dead, but of the living (Matthew 22:32 NRSV).

At the time the Lord made that statement to Moses, Abraham, Isaac and Jacob had been dead for hundreds of years. Yet God said that He "is" their God, not that He "was" their God. This means they were still alive in His presence though they had been physically dead for many years. This is another indication that there is a conscious existence for the believer after death.

5. BELIEVERS WILL LIVE TOGETHER WITH THE LORD

Paul told the church at Thessalonica that believers, once united with the Lord, will always be with Him. He put it this way.

> He died for us so that we can live with him forever, whether we are dead or alive at the time of his return (1 Thessalonians 5:10 NLT).

The wonderful promise is that believers will live together with the Lord for all of eternity.

6. THE INTERMEDIATE STATE IS A PLACE OF REST AND BLESSEDNESS

We also find something else from Scripture. Those who die in Jesus Christ are in a restful state. The Bible says.

> When He opened the fifth seal, I saw under the altar the souls of those slaughtered because of God's word and the testimony they had. They cried out with a loud voice: "O Lord, holy and true, how long until You judge and avenge our blood from those who live on the earth?" So a white robe was given to each of them, and they were told to rest a little while longer until [the number of] their fellow slaves and their brothers, who were going to be killed just as they had been, would be completed (Revelation 6:9-11 HCSB).

These martyrs, while in a restful state, needed to rest a little longer before the Lord avenged their death.

We also read that those with the Lord are said to be "blessed." The Book of Revelation puts it this way.

> And I heard a voice from heaven saying, "Write this: Blessed are the dead who die in the Lord from now on." "Blessed indeed," says the Spirit, "that they may rest from their labors, for their deeds follow them (Revelation 14:13 ESV).

The presence of the Lord is indeed a place of blessing.

7. THERE IS ACTIVITY IN THE INTERMEDIATE STATE

Though the intermediate state is a place of waiting, it is also a place of activity. We read about this in the Book of Revelation where it describes those believers who have died.

> That is why they are standing in front of the throne of God, serving him day and night in his Temple. And he who sits on the throne will live among them and shelter them (Revelation 7:15 NLT).

The intermediate state does not consist of inactivity. In fact, it is a place of service.

8. IT IS A PLACE OF HOLINESS

The believers who have died are presently in a state of holiness. In the Book of Revelation, the Apostle John asked an angel the identity of certain individuals. This angel gave the following answer to the prophet.

> And I said to him, "Sir, you know." So he said to me, "These are the ones who come out of the great tribulation, and washed their robes and made them white in the blood of the Lamb" (Revelation 7:14 NKJV).

The clothes that they are wearing, white robes, speak of holiness. They had been washed white with the blood of the lamb.

OTHER OBSERVATIONS ABOUT THE INTERMEDIATE STATE

There are other observations that need to be made about the intermediate state. They can be summed up as follows.

1. THERE IS AN EMPHASIS ON THE FINAL STATE

Though we have some information from the Bible concerning the intermediate state, it is not something that is emphasized. The hope of the believer is the coming of Jesus Christ. It is at that time the dead are raised in a glorified body, judged, and receive their rewards. The intermediate state is only a short interval between this life and the fullness of God's promises. Hence, this is the reason for the lack of emphasis on the intermediate state.

2. THERE IS A LIMITED AMOUNT REVEALED

In addition, the Bible only reveals a limited amount of information about what goes on in the presence of the Lord. Paul wrote of his experience.

I know a man in Christ who fourteen years ago was caught up to the third heaven. Whether it was in the body or out of the body I do not know—God knows. And I know that this man—whether in the body or apart from the body I do not know, but God knows—was caught up to paradise. He heard inexpressible things, things that man is not permitted to tell (2 Corinthians 12:2-4 NIV).

We find from these verses that Paul was not allowed to tell what he had experienced. If we knew exactly how wonderful it was, we probably would not be content to remain on the earth for one more hour. Being with the Lord will truly be an incredible experience!

SUMMARY TO QUESTION 5
TODAY, WHAT HAPPENS TO A BELIEVER IMMEDIATELY UPON DEATH?

Upon death, the soul, or spirit, of the believer goes immediately to be with the living God. Believers are alive and conscious in this state. In the Bible, there is no idea of a period of sleeping or waiting. The blessings of Christ are received immediately.

This is illustrated a number of ways in the New Testament. For example, Jesus told the criminal that was dying next to Him on the cross that he would be in paradise with the Lord that very day. There would be no waiting.

The martyr Stephen saw Jesus at the right hand of God the Father as he was being killed with stones. He asked the Lord Jesus to receive him. Again, being absent from this physical body allows the believer to immediately be with the Lord.

Paul told the Church at Corinth that to be absent from the body is to be immediately with the Lord. In other words, there is no waiting.

When Paul wrote to the Philippians he taught the same truth. He said that he had a desire to depart and to be with Christ. Paul said that this would be far better than anything he was presently experiencing.

These are some of the passages which teach that all Christians who die will go into God's presence without any delay upon their death. There is no waiting.

Though the intermediate state is not the place of our final reward, it is a place of rest, waiting, activity, and holiness. The Apostle Paul, who was caught up in the presence of the Lord in this unseen realm, wrote that he heard inexpressible things that a person is not allowed to communicate. In other words, the intermediate state is wonderful beyond any description!

Although believers have a natural curiosity about the intermediate state, Scripture focuses on the time when Jesus Christ returns. At that time He will raise and judge the dead, and then set up His everlasting kingdom. The Lord will then bless His people with such wonderful things; things that our minds presently cannot even imagine.

Do Believers Have A Body In Their Intermediate State?

From the time believers die, until they return to earth with Jesus Christ when He sets up His everlasting kingdom, they will be in some conscious form in the intermediate, or "in between" state. The Bible clearly teaches this.

However, there is the issue as to what form the believer will assume in the next world. Will we have a temporary body, be bodiless, or receive our eternal glorified body immediately upon death?

This question has been the object of much discussion among Bible believers. There are three main views as to what occurs to believers during this time in the intermediate state. They are as follows.

OPTION 1: BELIEVERS ARE DISEMBODIED SPIRITS

This view says that upon death the believer is conscious as a disembodied spirit. In other words, we are similar to angels, as well as other beings the Lord has created, who have no physical form. Our glorified body is received at the resurrection. This would mean each believer has an earthly body while alive, but have no body in the intermediate state, and then receive a glorified body at the resurrection of the dead. Thus, we will go through these three stages, body, bodiless, and then a final body.

OPTION 2: BELIEVERS HAVE A TEMPORARY BODY

Option two has the believer receiving a temporary body while waiting for their glorified body. We are not bodiless in heaven but we have not yet received our glorified body. This view sees the believer as always having a body; an earthly body in this life, an intermediate or temporary body upon death, and then finally a glorified body at the resurrection.

OPTION 3: BELIEVERS RECEIVE THEIR GLORIFIED BODY UPON DEATH

The third option says the believer receives their glorified body immediately at their death. There is no waiting for a general resurrection of the dead. Thus, the believer is in either one of two states; alive in this world with an earthly body or clothed with a glorified body in the next world.

THE ARGUMENTS FOR EACH VIEWPOINT

Those who hold each of these particular views believes that theirs is the best way to understand what the Bible says. We can set forth the case for each of these positions as follows.

OPTION 1: DEAD BELIEVERS ARE NOW DISEMBODIED SPIRITS

There are many Bible students who contend that, upon death, people who have believed in the Lord become conscious disembodied spirits awaiting the resurrection. There is certainly no need for a body in the realm of the dead. Since angels, as well as the other beings the Lord has created, the cherubim, seraphim and living creatures, function without bodies in the unseen world, then why can't believers do the same? Indeed, God Himself does not have a body!

Consequently there are three steps for the believer: this earthly body, a disembodied state after death, and finally a resurrected body when Christ returns. The disembodied state is far better than living in this body because the believer is with Christ. Yet it is short of all the things that God has promised. The arguments for this viewpoint are usually given as follows.

A. CHRIST WAS THE FIRST TO RECEIVE A NEW BODY

The Scripture says that Christ was the first to receive a resurrection body. Paul wrote the following to the church at Corinth.

> But now Christ has been raised from the dead, the first-fruits of those who have fallen asleep. For since death came through a man, the resurrection of the dead also comes through a man. For just as in Adam all die, so also in Christ all will be made alive. But each in his own order: Christ, the firstfruits; afterward, at His coming, the people of Christ (1 Corinthians 15:20-23 HCSB).

The righteous will receive their bodies sometime in the future. If the Old Testament saints had received their permanent body upon death, then Abraham, Moses, and the rest of the Old Testament believers, would have been resurrected and received a glorified body before Christ. But the Scripture says that Christ was the first. Consequently, they must not have received their permanent body upon their death.

B. MORE WILL BE TRANSFORMED AFTER HIM

In several passages, Paul makes it clear that the transformation of our bodies is still future. He wrote the following to the Thessalonians.

> For the Lord himself will come down from heaven with a commanding shout, with the voice of the archangel, and with the trumpet call of God. First, the Christians who have died will rise from their graves. Then, together with them, we who are still alive and remain on the earth will be caught up in the clouds to meet the Lord in the air. Then we will be with the Lord forever (1 Thessalonians 4:16,17 NLT).

This is a prediction about an event which is still future when Paul wrote to the Thessalonians. Indeed, it still has not happened.

He wrote about the instantaneous change to the Corinthians.

> It will happen in a moment, in the blinking of an eye, when the last trumpet is blown. For when the trumpet sounds, the Christians who have died will be raised with transformed bodies. And then we who are living will be transformed so that we will never die (1 Corinthians 15:52 NLT).

Again, this is a future event.

When Paul wrote to the Philippians he said that believers will have a glorious body like His. He stated it this way.

> But our citizenship is in heaven, and from it we await a Savior, the Lord Jesus Christ, who will transform our lowly body to be like his glorious body, by the power that enables him even to subject all things to himself (Philippians 3:20,21 ESV).

Thus, the righteous, the believers in Christ, do not receive their permanent bodies at death. This will have to wait until Jesus comes for His people. Hence, there is an interval of time between death and the resurrected state. Resurrection is in the future. It is "at the last trumpet." Until that time, believers are conscious in the presence of the Lord but they have yet received everything which God has promised.

C. THE NAKED OR UNCLOTHED STATE IS NOT TO BE DESIRED

There is also the statement which Paul makes about being unclothed. He wrote to the Corinthians explaining this unclothed state.

> Indeed, we who are in this tent groan, burdened as we are, because we do not want to be unclothed but clothed, so that mortality may be swallowed up by life (2 Corinthians 5:4 HCSB).

Paul said that he did not want to remain in a state where he was unclothed. Some understand this to mean that the intermediate state consists of being unclothed. Paul, therefore, is looking forward to the day when the intermediate state no longer exists and that he is clothed with the resurrection body which the Lord has promised those who believe.

These arguments have convinced many that the intermediate state is a state of disembodiment.

OPTION 2: BELIEVERS RECEIVE A TEMPORARY BODY AT DEATH

Another theory says that, at death, believers receive a temporary body in the in-between state. This is understood from what is taught in a number of places in Scripture.

Interestingly, the same statement of Paul which is used to argue that the in-between state is without a body is also used by others to say that the intermediate state consists of the believer having a temporary body. He wrote.

> For we who are in *this* tent groan, being burdened, not because we want to be unclothed, but further clothed, that mortality may be swallowed up by life (2 Corinthians 5:4 NKJV).

It is argued that Paul's desire was to be clothed with some temporary, intermediate body upon his death. He did not want to be in a disembodied state. The naked state was an unsatisfactory state. Therefore, there would not be any time in the future when he would be unclothed or without a body.

Consequently, upon death, he was looking for some temporary body until the resurrection of the dead. According to this view, the believer would always have some type of body. The three step process would be: an earthly body, a temporary body, and then a glorified body. The glorified body only comes at the resurrection of the dead.

Several other biblical arguments are usually given for this viewpoint.

LAZARUS, ABRAHAM AND THE RICH MAN HAD BODIES

In the story of the rich man and Lazarus it seems that both of these dead individuals were in some type of body. The rich man said to Abraham.

> And he called out, 'Father Abraham, have mercy on me, and send Lazarus to dip the end of his finger in water and cool my tongue, for I am in anguish in this flame' (Luke 16:24 ESV).

It would not seem to make sense for the rich man to ask Lazarus, whom he could see, to come and dip his finger in water and cool the tongue of this suffering rich man if Lazarus did not have a finger and the rich man did not have a tongue! Consequently, some type of body seems to be in view here. Otherwise the request seems meaningless.

MOSES AND ELIJAH APPEARED IN BODIES

When Moses and Elijah appeared at Jesus' transfiguration, there is every indication that they appeared in some type of bodily form. They were recognizable by the three men who were with Jesus; Peter, James, and John. Again, this seems to indicate that they had their same bodily form, or at least a similar bodily form, in the realm of the dead as they had here upon the earth. In other words, they were immediately recognizable.

RESPONSE

While these passages may indeed indicate that there is some type of intermediate body, they are not decisive. For one thing, it seems that Jesus, in His intermediate state between His death on the cross and His resurrection from the dead, was a bodiless spirit. We know His body was in the grave.

In an admittedly difficult passage, Peter may be indicating that Jesus' spirit, without a body, preached to the spirits of the dead. He wrote.

> For Christ also suffered once for sins, the righteous for the unrighteous, that he might bring us to God, being put to

death in the flesh but made alive in the spirit, in which he went
and proclaimed to the spirits in prison (1 Peter 3:18,19 ESV).

Jesus was put to death in His flesh, His body, but His spirit remained alive. This passage is understood to mean that His spirit preached to other spirits in the realm of the dead while His body was in the grave for three days. This would seem to indicate that the dead exist as "spirits" without bodies.

However, this is a difficult passage and it is certainly not clear that this is the correct interpretation of these verses. In fact, we think there is a much better understanding of this passage (see our book *Hell: The Final Destination For Unbelievers*, Appendix 5).

OPTION 3: BELIEVERS RECEIVE A GLORIFIED BODY AT DEATH

There is also the view that the believer receives their glorified body upon death. In other words, they are instantaneously resurrected. This position says there is no waiting period between death and the new body that God has promised believers. The biblical support for this belief is found in 2 Corinthians 5:1-10. It is thought that Paul teaches in this passage that the resurrected body is received upon death.

> For we know that if the earthly tent we live in is destroyed,
> we have a building from God, a house not made with hands,
> eternal in the heavens (2 Corinthians 5:1 NRSV).

This passage is used to teach that a glorified body is received immediately upon death. There is no waiting, no intermediate body.

A. THERE IS NO DISEMBODIED STATE

According to this understanding of what Paul wrote, there is no disembodied state between the destruction of our present earthly house, our earthly bodies, and God's provision of an eternal house, a heavenly body. Consequently, there is no fear of being unclothed.

Therefore, when the earthly tent is destroyed, believers immediately receive their new, God-made building; their glorified body. Resurrection is, therefore, immediate.

While the resurrection of the dead in the afterlife does indeed occur immediately upon death, it remains hidden from public view. It will only be revealed when Jesus Christ appears a second time. Paul wrote.

> When the Messiah, who is your life, is revealed, then you also will be revealed with Him in glory (Colossians 3:4 HCSB).

This statement is understood to mean that believers will be *revealed* with their resurrected bodies when Christ comes. They will not "receive" them at that time.

B. WHY SHOULD BELIEVERS WAIT FOR THE RESURRECTION BODY?

It is also argued that there is no reason for the believer to wait for their resurrection body. If the believer will ultimately receive a glorified body, then why is there the wait? Since they are already conscious in heaven in the presence of Christ, why must they wait to receive what He has promised? There does not seem to be any reason for this.

C. THERE IS NO UNDERSTANDING OF TIME IN THE UNSEEN WORLD

Furthermore, those in the intermediate state would have no understanding of time as we know it. Since there is no real reason for them to wait to receive their glorified body, it is argued that God gives it to them immediately upon their death.

D. AT SECOND COMING ALL WILL BE BROUGHT TOGETHER, NOT RAISED

Therefore, at the Second Coming of Jesus Christ to the earth, all the resurrected saints are brought together and publicly displayed, not raised from the dead at that time.

RESPONSE

The problem with this view is that it seems to flatly contradict 1 Thessalonians 4 and 1 Corinthians 15 with respect to the time of the new bodies for the believers. Both these passages emphasize the old bodies of all believers will be changed when Christ returns, not before. To Paul, the resurrection of the body is something future for everyone.

Jesus also said the dead will be raised in the future. We read the following words of our Lord in the Gospel of John.

> And I assure you that the time is coming, in fact it is here, when the dead will hear my voice—the voice of the Son of God. And those who listen will live. The Father has life in himself, and he has granted his Son to have life in himself. And he has given him authority to judge all mankind because he is the Son of Man. Don't be so surprised! Indeed, the time is coming when all the dead in their graves will hear the voice of God's Son, and they will rise again. Those who have done good will rise to eternal life, and those who have continued in evil will rise to judgment (John 5:25-29 NLT).

This seems to refute the idea that the resurrection body is received immediately upon death. Believers are still waiting for the resurrection of the body.

Therefore, the intermediate state is only a temporary state between the time the believer dies and when he or she receives their resurrected body.

OBSERVATION: THE NEW TESTAMENT IS NOT THAT CONCERNED ABOUT THE INTERMEDIATE STATE

There is an important matter about the in-between state that must be understood; it is not an significant topic as far as the New Testament writers are concerned. The New Testament is not that clear as to the form of the dead in the intermediate state. The main concern of the Bible is with the ultimate destiny of believers and their glorified body. A statement from Paul can sum up the biblical attitude.

> If we live, we live to the Lord, and if we die, we die to the Lord; so then, whether we live or whether we die, we are the Lord's (Romans 14:8 NRSV).

Ultimately all believers are with the Lord upon death and are enjoying wonderful surroundings. Beyond this we cannot be certain as to what form they now have.

SUMMARY TO QUESTION 6
DO BELIEVERS HAVE A BODY IN THEIR INTERMEDIATE STATE?

It is clear from the Scripture that believers immediately go into the presence of Jesus Christ upon death. As to what form we have in the intermediate state, it is not that obvious. Bible-believing Christians hold to three different views.

Some Christians teach that all believers are disembodied spirits upon death. In other words, we are similar to angels, and other beings whom the Lord created, who can function in the unseen realm without a body. Our glorified body comes at the time of the resurrection of the dead. This would mean we would move from a body here upon the earth to a bodiless state upon death and finally to a glorified body at the resurrection. Thus, there is a body, no body, and then a body.

Other Bible-believers think some type of temporary body is given to all believers at death. The believer does not receive their resurrection body immediately upon death, rather they will be in some temporary form until given their eternal body. This means we would always have a body no matter what state we are in. We go from a human body, to a temporary body, to a glorified body.

Finally, there are others who see no need for waiting for a glorified body. They think that God gives each believer his or her new body upon death. There is no waiting period.

In truth, the Bible is not overly concerned about the state of the believer before the resurrection. Instead, it emphasizes the resurrected and glorified state. Consequently, any conclusions we hold about what our body may or may not be like in the intermediate state can only be held tentatively. There is no decisive answer to this question.

Do Believers Experience All God's Promises In The Intermediate State?

Between this life and eternity is what is known as the intermediate state. The word intermediate means "between the times." Indeed, it is a state of being between our time here upon the earth and the eternal realm.

Because this is an "in-between" state there is a certain amount of incompleteness. All of the promises of God are not experienced in the intermediate state. Indeed, the intermediate state is incomplete for the believer in at least three ways.

1. THE BODY OF CHRIST, THE CHURCH, REMAINS INCOMPLETE

The church, or the body of Christ, is presently incomplete. This will be the case until the last person enters into the body of Christ by believing in Jesus as their Savior.

The writer to the Hebrews noted this. After explaining the righteous deeds of many of the biblical characters in the Old Testament, he made the following conclusion.

> All these people earned a good reputation because of their faith, yet none of them received all that God had promised. For God had something better in mind for us, so that they would not reach perfection without us (Hebrews 11:39,40 NLT).

The ones which have gone before us will not be made perfect or complete without us. While technically these Old Testament saints are not part of what is known as the "body of Christ," the church, the principle is still the same

At that time, when all the believers in Jesus Christ are together, the intermediate state will end. Believers will be raised in their new bodies, receive their rewards, and then Christ will return to judge the people of the earth.

2. BELIEVERS DO NOT HAVE A GLORIFIED BODY

The intermediate state of the believer is incomplete in the sense that their body has not been glorified. Whether the believer remains disembodied, or has some sort of temporary body in the intermediate state, the final glorified body has not yet been given. Believers are still waiting to receive this promised body.

3. THE DEAD ARE LIMITED TO HEAVEN

Those in the intermediate state are presently limited to heaven. However, the earth also belongs to those who have believed in God's promises. The Lord has promised that He will put His kingdom upon the earth. Yet the earth is still in a state of sin waiting the time when Christ returns and deals with the sin problem.

In fact, the Lord will eventually create a new heaven and new earth, a new universe. We read about this in the Book of Revelation.

> Then I saw a new heaven and a new earth, for the old heaven and the old earth had disappeared. And the sea was also gone. And I saw the holy city, the new Jerusalem, coming down from God out of heaven like a bride beautifully dressed for her husband (Revelation 21:1-2 NLT).

Therefore, a new universe awaits the deceased believers.

THERE IS NOT A TOTAL CONTRAST BETWEEN THE TWO STATES

The intermediate state, however, does have much in common with the final state. In other words, there is not a total contrast between the two. It is basically a transitional place from the earthly existence to the heavenly with many of the benefits of heaven.

DO THEY GO STRAIGHT TO THE FINAL RESTING PLACE?

As we observed in question one, there are some who deny that any intermediate state exists for the believer or unbeliever. This view holds that the spirits of the dead go to their final resting place upon death. When Scripture speaks of judgment and resurrection, they believe that it is only figurative. They say that each individual is judged at death. For this particular viewpoint, death and resurrection would then be identical.

RESPONSE

This view has to spiritualize the plain teaching of the Scripture on the subject, as well as reinterpret the events around the Second Coming of Christ. There is no warrant for understanding what the Bible has to say about the death, resurrection, judgment and the coming of Christ in anything but a literal manner.

OBSERVATION: THE RESURRECTION OF THE DEAD MAKES AN INTERMEDIATE STATE NECESSARY

The fact that there will be a future resurrection and then an ultimate judgment makes some type of "in-between" or "intermediate state necessary. After each person dies, they await the final judgment of God. This seems to be the obvious conclusion which we can make from Scripture.

SUMMARY TO QUESTION 7
DO BELIEVERS EXPERIENCE ALL GOD'S PROMISES IN THE INTERMEDIATE STATE?

The intermediate state is an in-between state. By definition, this state does not provide the believer with everything that God has promised.

In other words, it is incomplete. While it is much greater for the believer than our present earthly existence, it is still incomplete for a number of reasons.

For one thing, the believing dead are still waiting for the church, the body of Christ, to be complete. There are still more believers to join these saints in the afterlife. The church, His body, waits to be completed.

The glorified body of each and every believer is not received until the time of the resurrection of the dead. Whatever particular form the believing dead may presently have, it is not the glorified body which God has promised them. This will occur for all believers simultaneously at the resurrection of the dead. Until then, no believer will receive his or her eternal body.

As of this time, the believing dead only have access to heaven, not to earth. Eventually they will access to the entire universe.

Furthermore, the universe to which they will have access will be renewed. All traces of sin will be removed. Indeed, an entire new universe will be created.

There are some that teach that no intermediate state exists; both believer and unbeliever alike go immediately to their final reward. However, the fact that there will be a resurrection someday of both the wicked and the righteous, and a final judgment, makes an intermediate state absolutely necessary. Consequently, there remain certain promises which the Lord has made to believers which are still to be fulfilled.

Does The Soul Of The Believer Develop Morally Or Spiritually In The Intermediate State?

The Bible teaches that the intermediate state is a conscious state. Those who have died are immediately with Jesus Christ in complete consciousness. The Scripture is clear about this.

The fact that believers are conscious in this state brings up a question. Does that believer develop or grow spiritually while in the in-between state? Some people assume we will indeed develop spiritually. Instead of being a state where all growth or development stops, they see the in-between state as a time the person grows morally.

Is this what is going to occur? What does the Bible have to say about this matter?

SCRIPTURE IS SILENT ON THIS ISSUE

While it may be possible for some type of growth or development in the in-between or intermediate state, the Bible is completely silent on the matter. We do not know, one way or the other, if there is any spiritual growth for the believing dead. If the Bible is silent then we should not speculate. We simply do not know the answer.

REWARDS ARE BASED UPON THINGS DONE ON EARTH

While we are not told if there is any spiritual development in the intermediate state, we do know that any rewards believers will receive will be based upon the things done while here on the earth. The New Testament makes this clear.

Indeed, Paul wrote to the Corinthians about the rewards we will receive when we appear before Christ. They will be based upon what we have done on this earth and in this body. He explained it this way.

> According to God's grace that was given to me, as a skilled master builder I have laid a foundation, and another builds on it. But each one must be careful how he builds on it, because no one can lay any other foundation than what has been laid—that is, Jesus Christ. If anyone builds on the foundation with gold, silver, costly stones, wood, hay, or straw, each one's work will become obvious, for the day will disclose it, because it will be revealed by fire; the fire will test the quality of each one's work. If anyone's work that he has built survives, he will receive a reward. If anyone's work is burned up, it will be lost, but he will be saved; yet it will be like an escape through (1 Corinthians 3:10-15 HCSB).

The rewards we will receive from Christ will be based upon what we do in this life alone. Even if it is possible for us to grow spiritually in the intermediate state there will not be any rewards for this potential growth.

WE WILL LEARN NEW THINGS IN ETERNITY

Though the Bible does not give us an answer about spiritual growth or development in the intermediate realm, we do know that we will be learning new things in the eternal state. Paul wrote the following to the Ephesians.

> So that in the coming ages He might display the immeasurable riches of His grace in [His] kindness to us in Christ Jesus (Ephesians 2:7 HCSB).

The fact that God will display His immeasurable riches to us for all eternity certainly suggests that we will be constantly learning new things. Therefore, our knowledge will continue to increase. However, this says nothing about our spiritual or moral development.

The fact that we will be like Christ, and perfected in our glorified bodies, may indicate that we will not need to grow spiritually. Yet, since there is still so much we do not know about the unseen realm it is best that we don't come to any firm conclusions.

As we have emphasized, Scripture is more interested in our eternal state than it is in any intermediate or in-between state. Consequently, there are many things which we are not told about this intermediate state and there is still much we do not know about the eternal state. However, what we do know about our future, as believers, is truly wonderful!

SUMMARY TO QUESTION 8
DOES THE SOUL OF THE BELIEVER DEVELOP MORALLY OR SPIRITUALLY IN THE INTERMEDIATE STATE?

While the spirit, or soul, is completely conscious in the intermediate state there is no indication that it is a time of spiritual growth or development. While many people wonder if we will grow spiritually in the in-between state, the Bible is silent on this issue. Since Scripture is silent it would not be wise for us to speculate on what may or may not happen. For whatever reason, God has not answered this question.

We do know that the rewards we will receive at the judgment seat of Christ will be based upon what we do in this life alone. Indeed, our rewards will be given based upon our earthly behavior. It will all depend upon how faithful we have been to Jesus Christ in this life.

Whether or not we develop or grow in the in-between state will have no meaning upon our eternal rewards. This we do know. Beyond this, we cannot say.

The Bible does tell us that there will be intellectual growth and development for us in the eternal state. In fact, the Bible emphasizes that the riches of the Lord will be displayed to us for all eternity. This assumes that we will continually be learning new things.

However, whether this means that we will also grow spiritually is another matter. Scripture does not seem to touch on this issue. Therefore, no conclusive answer can be given.

QUESTION 9

What Is The Intermediate State
For The Unbeliever?

As is true with the believer, the unbeliever also goes to a temporary place upon their death. Therefore, the resurrection and final judgment of the wicked is not immediate. Before that future time, there is an "in between" state where the unbeliever is waiting to be judged. What happens to them in the meantime?

THE OLD TESTAMENT SAYS THEY WENT TO SHEOL

When an unbelieving person died during Old Testament times, their body, like the body of the believer, went to a place called Sheol. The basic meaning of Sheol is the grave, the place where bodies are buried. Thus, believer and unbeliever alike went to Sheol.

There are some Old Testament passages that speak of Sheol welcoming the dead. Some have interpreted this to mean Sheol is also a place where the spirits of the dead await future judgment. Thus, Sheol may also refer to the unseen realm of the dead where the spirits of the dead reside.

THE NEW TESTAMENT SAYS THEY WENT TO HADES

The New Testament provides more information for us about the in-between state of the unbeliever. While the body of the unbeliever went to the grave, their spirit, or soul, went to the unseen realm of the dead. This place is called Hades in the New Testament. It says the following about the intermediate state of the unbeliever.

1. THEY ARE IN PRISON

The spirits of the unbelieving dead are in prison and are under guard. Peter wrote the following about these spirits.

> So he went and preached to the spirits in prison (1 Peter 3:19 NLT).

These spirits are said to be in prison. The idea is that they cannot escape their confinement. They have been jailed for their sins.

2. THEY ARE UNDER JUDGMENT

Those who have died outside of the Lord are now under His judgment. The writer to the Hebrews noted that judgment comes after death.

> And just as it is destined that each person dies only once and after that comes judgment (Hebrews 9:27 NLT).

Judgment is waiting for these people. There is no escaping this.

3. THEY ARE SUFFERING PUNISHMENT

In the Gospel of Luke, Jesus told the story of the rich man and Lazarus. This account gives us insight into the intermediate state of the wicked dead. Therefore, it is important that we look at the entire story our Lord gave so that we can make some observations about the in-between state. It reads as follows.

> There was a rich man who was dressed in purple and fine linen and lived in luxury every day. At his gate was laid a beggar named Lazarus, covered with sores and longing to eat what fell from the rich man's table. Even the dogs came and licked his sores. The time came when the beggar died and the angels carried him to Abraham's side. The rich man also died and was buried. In hell, where he was in torment, he looked up and saw Abraham far away, with Lazarus by his

side. So he called to him, 'Father Abraham, have pity on me and send Lazarus to dip the tip of his finger in water and cool my tongue, because I am in agony in this fire.' But Abraham replied, 'Son, remember that in your lifetime you received your good things, while Lazarus received bad things, but now he is comforted here and you are in agony. And besides all this, between us and you a great chasm has been fixed, so that those who want to go from here to you cannot, nor can anyone cross over from there to us.' He answered, 'Then I beg you, father, send Lazarus to my father's house, for I have five brothers. Let him warn them, so that they will not also come to this place of torment.' Abraham replied, 'They have Moses and the Prophets; let them listen to them.' 'No, father Abraham,' he said, 'but if someone from the dead goes to them, they will repent.' He said to him, 'If they do not listen to Moses and the Prophets, they will not be convinced even if someone rises from the dead' (Luke 16:19-31 NIV).

The rich man was in a conscious place of torment, a place of punishment. He suffered such things as loneliness and thirst. He was obviously able to experience pain. Therefore, the intermediate state for the unbeliever is a place of punishment.

These passages tell us something of the present state of all unbelievers who have died. It is truly a horrifying place to be.

THEY ARE AWAITING THE DAY OF JUDGMENT

Unbelievers are now in a temporary place of judgment. Peter wrote about an eventual judgment that the unrighteous will face.

The Lord knows how to rescue the godly from trials and to hold the unrighteous for punishment on the day of judgment (2 Peter 2:9).

There will be a punishment, after a final judgment for those unbelievers. This is something which the Bible makes very clear. Indeed, there is no escaping this coming destiny.

SUMMARY TO QUESTION 9
WHAT IS THE INTERMEDIATE STATE FOR THE UNBELIEVER?

The Bible teaches that there is an intermediate state for those who have believed in Jesus Christ. The righteous dead are being comforted in this state. This is one of the many promises the Lord has given to Christians. Upon death, we have the hope of being instantly in a blissful state.

There is also an intermediate or "in between" state for the unbeliever. Between their death and resurrection, their body remains in the grave while their spirit, or soul, is in the unseen realm of the dead awaiting final judgment. From Scripture, we learn certain things about this state.

For one thing, they are in prison. In other words, they are in a place of temporary confinement.

In addition, they are awaiting the final judgment of God while they are in this temporary prison.

Furthermore, we find that they are already suffering punishment before the time of their final judgment. Jesus made this clear in His story of the rich man and Lazarus. This teaches us that immediately upon death unbelievers are experiencing punishment for their rejection of Christ. There is no waiting period, no period of unconsciousness or sleep. Immediate punishment is their destiny once they leave this world. In other words, there is no rest for the wicked.

Was Jesus' Story Of The Rich Man And Lazarus A Parable?

There has been much debate about the story that Jesus told of the rich man and Lazarus (Luke 16). Is it merely a parable, a non-actual story, that is meant to teach us certain truths? Or is it citing a genuine event that happened in the afterlife?

In addition, whether or not it is an actual story of something that truly happened, does it give us specific information about the in-between state of those who have died? In other words, should we carefully examine it to determine what existence is like for those in the afterlife?

There are good Bible-believers who debate these questions.

ARGUMENTS FOR IT BEING A TRUE STORY

Many believe the account of the rich man and Lazarus is actually a true story. In other words, we are dealing with two real persons who died and their fate is recorded for us. Consequently, we can learn many things about the afterlife because we are dealing with genuine events. The arguments given that it is more than a parable are as follows.

1. TWO CHARACTERS IN THE STORY ARE NAMED

If this is a parable, it is the only one where people are named; Lazarus and Abraham. The fact that these people are named seems to tell us that this is more than a mere parable; an earthly story with a heavenly meaning. In all true parables the people remain nameless or belong to general categories of people such as the Levite and the Good Samaritan. Yet in this story we have specific names.

2. IT IS NOT INTRODUCED AS A PARABLE

The account is not introduced as a parable. Often, though not always, Jesus made it clear that He was giving a parable. Indeed, either Jesus or the gospel writer who recorded the story, state in a matter of fact manner that this is a parable. Yet we find nothing like that stated in the account of the rich man and Lazarus.

3. FIVE BROTHERS ARE MENTIONED

In addition, the rich man told Abraham that he had five brothers who were still living upon the earth. Why mention this specific number if it is only a parable? This seems to be a further reason as to why this should be considered a true story.

4. ALL OTHER PARABLES WERE ABOUT THIS LIFE

All the parables Jesus taught were about everyday life in this world, not the afterlife. This would be the one exception if it is a true parable. While other parables speak of a coming judgment or wedding banquet for the believers, this particular story gives us specific details of life in the next world, life in the in-between state.

Therefore, we have reasons to believe that the story that Jesus told of the rich man and Lazarus, as recorded in Luke's gospel, was an actual occurrence.

ARGUMENTS FOR BELIEVING IT IS MERELY A PARABLE

While many people think that the story of the rich man and Lazarus was a record of events which really happened, there are also a number of arguments for it being a parable. The following points are usually made by those who believe we are dealing with a parable rather than real events.

1. NOT EVERY PARABLE IS INTRODUCED AS A PARABLE

The fact that Jesus does not state that this is a parable is not decisive. There are a number of parables which are not introduced as such. For example, in the same gospel, Luke, we find this happening. Indeed, in Luke 15, there are a series of parables but only the first one is introduced as a genuine parable.

2. THE PHRASE "A CERTAIN MAN" IS OFTEN USED IN JESUS' PARABLES

Another argument for it being a parable is Jesus use of the introductory phrase, "A certain man." This is consistent of how Jesus introduced true parables.

3. THE SUBJECT HE IS ADDRESSING IS RICHES, NOT THE AFTERLIFE

There is also the argument that the point of Jesus' parable is not what life is going to be life in the next world but rather about the misuse of riches in this life. From this, some conclude that we should not press the details of the story. In other words, Jesus is not attempting to give us specific details about what happens after people die.

However, this line of reasoning does not follow at all. Even if the main subject of the parable is the misuse of riches, this should not preclude us from drawing inferences about the afterlife from some of the other statements of Jesus in this story. The fact that He gave us so many specific details should cause us to take them seriously and not ignore them.

IT STILL PROVIDES INFORMATION ABOUT THE AFTERLIFE

In sum, no matter how we understand this account of the rich man and Lazarus it does provide us with certain details of the afterlife which we should assume are true. Indeed, the fact that Jesus has given us a number of specifics about life in the next world is something which Bible-believers should take seriously. We should not ignore His teaching here.

SUMMARY TO QUESTION 10

WAS JESUS' STORY OF THE RICH MAN AND LAZARUS A PARABLE?

There is a question as to how to understand the story that Jesus told about the rich man and Lazarus. Are we dealing with real people and their genuine experiences in the next world, or was it a parable, a story that is not speaking of an actual situation in the afterlife? Christians are divided on this issue. Indeed, there is no consensus as to how to understand it.

There seem to be a number of facts that would suggest that it is more than a parable. First, two people are named; Lazarus and Abraham. In none of Jesus' parables do we find personal names of individuals. The characters are either nameless or belong to generic categories such as priests, Levites or Samaritans.

Second, the account is not specifically introduced as a parable. Most of Jesus' parables are introduced to us in that manner. In other words, we are told that this is a parable. The fact that this story is not introduced as a parable seems to give us further indication that we are dealing with actual history, not a mere story to teach us certain truths.

Third, there are a specific number of brothers mentioned; five. This is another reason as to why we are looking at actual events instead of some parable.

Finally, this is the only story that Jesus told which is solely about the afterlife. This sets it apart from His parables which deal with life in the everyday world.

Those who argue for it to be a parable or a parable-like story say that not every parable of Jesus is introduced as such. Therefore, the fact that it is not introduced that way is not conclusive.

Furthermore, Jesus began the story with the phrase, "A certain man." This is how He often introduced other parables. Thus, some people take the story as representative of what goes on in the afterlife but not as a specific event which happened to two individuals upon their deaths.

Others reject the historicity of the story by noting the entire story is not about the afterlife but rather about the misuse of riches. Therefore, the details of Lazarus and the rich man in the next world are not meant to be an actual report of what goes on in the unseen realm.

However, this line of reasoning does not follow. Even if it were a parable, which is debated, the fact that Jesus gave a number of details about the next world should cause us to take what He taught seriously. Indeed, there are reasons as to why He has provided so much detail.

We conclude that whether of not this is an actual account of something which occurred in the afterlife, the details provided in this story should be accepted as being a factual representation of what truly goes on in the unseen world in the intermediate state of the dead.

Consequently, we can, and we should, learn a number of important truths about the next world from this story Jesus told.

What Can Be Learned About The Afterlife From The Account Of The Rich Man And Lazarus? (Luke 16:19-31)

Among other reasons, Jesus gave us the story of the rich man and Lazarus to illustrate what conditions are like in the afterlife. In this account there are a number of things that we learn about life in the unseen world for those who have died. They include the following truths.

1. THE DEAD DO NOT GO OUT OF EXISTENCE

This account teaches us that both the godly and the ungodly survive after death. They do not become non-existent. There is life after death. This is consistent with what we know from other parts of Scripture.

2. THE DEAD GO TO AN ACTUAL PLACE

We also learn that there was an definite place where the immaterial part of us, the spirit, actually goes. Death is followed by a destination. Thus, there is some tangible spot where the dead gather. They are somewhere.

3. THE DEAD DO NOT ALL GO TO THE SAME PLACE

Though the dead go to an actual place, they do not all go to the same place. Jesus said the rich man was in Hades while Lazarus was in the bosom of Abraham. Consequently, everyone who dies goes to one of two specific destinations.

4. THE DEAD ARE CONSCIOUS

There is no idea of annihilation, or extinction, of the individual in the next world. This rich man was completely conscious in this place of punishment. Indeed, he knew who he was, and that he had five brothers who were still living. He also knew who Abraham was, as well as knowing the identity of Lazarus.

Furthermore, he knew where he was. He was in Hades separated from the Lord, and he certainly knew why he was there; he was disobedient to the Lord in his life. He also got a glimpse of the righteous dead living in comfort. In all of this the rich man was completely conscious at all times.

5. THE DEAD HAVE ALL THEIR SENSES

We find that the rich man had all his senses in Hades. He could see Abraham and Lazarus, he recognized their individual identity, and he could hear Abraham speak as well as communicate with him. In addition, he could also feel pain and experience suffering.

6. THE DEAD RETAIN THEIR MEMORY

The rich man was in complete possession of his memory. While in the torment of Hades he was concerned about his five brothers that were still upon the earth. He also recognized Lazarus, the beggar who had been at his gate, as well as the patriarch. Abraham. In addition, Abraham told the rich man to remember how he treated Lazarus while both of them were alive. This further indicates that this man had a clear memory of the past.

This fact teaches us some important truths. The unsaved dead remember their past. They realize why they end up at their destination in the unseen world. Furthermore, the unbelieving dead remember all the lost opportunities which were given them in this life to believe God and follow His Word. They will have all eternity to think about this!

7. THE RIGHTEOUS DEAD ARE NAMED, THE UNRIGHTEOUS ARE UNNAMED

Another interesting fact that we learn here, as well as elsewhere in Scripture, is that the righteous dead are named. In other words, their unique identity is recognized by others.

However, nowhere in the Bible are unbelievers named in the next life. The person in this story is merely called "the rich man." The unrighteous dead, though still existing, are never acknowledged as individual persons.

8. THERE WAS CROSSING OVER TO THE OTHER SIDE

Once a person is dead then their fate has been forever sealed. Jesus made it clear there was no crossing over from one side of the realm of the dead to the other side. In other words, the unrighteous can never join the righteous and the righteous can never visit the unrighteous. There is a chasm between them which cannot be bridged. Destinies are not reversible. This is what we learn from this story.

9. THERE IS NO SECOND CHANCE TO RIGHT OUR WRONGS

There is no returning from the dead to try to correct wrong decisions which were made in this life. There is no second chance, no crossing over from the next world back into ours. The rich man could not even warn his family of their impending fate. In sum, what we do in this life determines our destiny in the next.

10. APPEAL TO PERSONAL HERITAGE CANNOT CHANGE THINGS

The rich man appealed to "Father" Abraham to have mercy upon him. Perhaps he thought his heritage as a Jew would gain him favor. However, this was not the case. John the Baptist had earlier warned the Jews about attempting to do this. He gave the following warning to the religious leaders who were assuming that God would not judge them because Abraham was their ancestor. Luke records his words.

Produce fruit in keeping with repentance. And do not begin to say to yourselves, 'We have Abraham as our father.' For I tell you that out of these stones God can raise up children for Abraham (Luke 3:8 NIV).

Personal heritage means nothing as far as the afterlife is concerned. Each of us must individually trust the God of the Bible in this life so that we will be in His presence in the next life.

11. THERE WAS NO REST, NO PEACE, FOR THE WICKED DEAD

The rich man was continually in torment in this place. He had not rest, no peace, whatsoever. He was consciously suffering this punishment and there was no end to his suffering. This reaffirms a biblical principle.

"There is no peace," says the Lord, "for the wicked" (Isaiah 48:22 NIV).

12. THE WICKED DEAD HAVE UNFILLED DESIRES

The place of torment is a place of thirst. This speaks of unfulfilled desire. It is also a sign of God's judgment. Quenching thirst in the Old Testament symbolized desiring God's presence.

However, this rich man would not experience the personal presence of God. Those in this horrible place have desires that cannot be met. Indeed, there were no crumbs for the rich man to eat, no water for his parched throat. He received all of the good things in this life but did not use them wisely. Now he has an unfulfilled desire for these good things. Unfortunately, he will never receive them. His fate has been forever sealed.

13. THE THINGS FROM THIS LIFE CANNOT BE TAKEN INTO THE NEXT WORLD

In this life, the rich man was envied while Lazarus was looked down upon as a person in a desperate situation. However, living a life without

God does not ultimately satisfy. The riches this particular man had in this life did not make any difference whatsoever in the next. Likewise the poverty that Lazarus experienced in this life was not carried over to the next.

This is an important truth. It was thought by many at the time of Jesus that earthly riches were a sign of God's blessing and that poverty was a sign of God's judgment. We find from this story of Jesus that this is not always the case.

In fact, the situation of the rich man and Lazarus was reversed in the afterlife. Lazarus who suffered in this life was rewarded in the next while the rich man who lived in luxury his entire life suffered in the afterlife. Consequently, our present state is no indication of our position in the afterlife.

14. THE RICH MAN HAD A FALSE IDEA OF WHAT CAN HAPPEN

The rich man acted as if nothing had changed. He had the false idea that Lazarus could be a messenger to his five brothers. Yet Jesus made it clear that no messengers can come from the next world to visit this world.

Thus, we should not attempt to contact the dead to get any specific details of the afterlife. This includes trying to contact deceased believers. They are not allowed to give us any information about the next life. This is reserved for God's Word and for it alone. Only the truth of God's Word could rescue his family from the same fate.

15. THE WICKED DEAD ARE IN ANGUISH AND CRY OUT

The intermediate state of the unbeliever is also a place of intense pain. The word torment is used five times in this account. While they cry for help there is no one to help them. They are alone in their torment. This further illustrates the horrible punishment which these people are experiencing.

16. THE WICKED DEAD ARE SEPARATED FROM EVERYTHING

This illustrates our next point. The rich man was separated from everything, both good and evil, in the afterlife. He was by himself in total isolation. There was no one to whom he could communicate about his sufferings. The punishment for the wicked will consist of complete loneliness. He realized this horrible truth too late.

17. THE WICKED ARE WITHOUT HOPE

The man realized that he was not ever going to leave the place of punishment. He was completely without hope. He would have to spend all of eternity in this miserable state where he was separated from the Lord. A worse fate cannot be imagined.

18. PEOPLE ARE ACCOUNTABLE CONCERNING HOW THEY USE MONEY

The rich man ate well, dressed well and knew Lazarus was suffering at his gate. But he did not care. He was held accountable for his poor treatment of this helpless beggar. He should have helped him but he did not. He is now paying the price for that indifference.

19. THE UNRIGHTEOUS DEAD DO NOT WANT OTHERS TO JOIN THEM

We learn that those being punished in the unseen realm of the dead do not want their friends and relatives to join them. The rich man in Jesus' story wanted the beggar Lazarus to return to warn his five brothers of the fate which awaited them. He would rather never see them again than have these five people suffer the same tragic end as he was suffering.

Consequently, it seems that some feeling of concern for the living remains with the unbelieving dead. This is so ironic. The unbelieving dead are interested in the gospel message going out!

20. ABRAHAM WAS AWARE OF CERTAIN THINGS

In the righteous part of the unseen world, we find that Abraham was aware of Moses as well as the prophets who came after him in history.

This shows that the righteous dead have an idea of time and history. To some degree, their memory remains with them in the afterlife.

21. EVEN ONE RETURNING FROM THE DEAD WILL NOT CAUSE PEOPLE TO BELIEVE

The rich man assumed that people would believe if someone came back from the dead to warn them of what lies ahead for unbelievers. He insisted that signs and wonders are necessary for people to believe. Someone who has died knows the answer to the question of human destiny. This, he thought, would convince his five brothers.

Yet Abraham said that even a voice from the dead would not convince someone. Indeed, nobody could not bring a clearer message about the afterlife than the message Scripture already brings.

22. THE SCRIPTURES ARE ENOUGH

The rich man had the false belief that the miracle of Lazarus' returning would cause his brothers to repent. Jesus emphasized the Word of God is sufficient to cause people to believe. The Scriptures are sufficient. We do not need anything else. This is a powerful statement on the sufficiency of the Word of God. God has spoken but the problem is that people are not listening.

The irony of this is that someone did indeed come back from the dead, the teller of this story, Jesus Christ. Even so, people still do not believe. The resurrection of Jesus Christ is not sufficient, in and of itself, to cause someone to believe if they do not wish to believe.

Indeed, people must be willing to hear the gospel message and believe in Christ. Unhappily, too many people do not want to hear about Jesus and, consequently, are cutting themselves off from any hope of heaven and eternal happiness.

23. THE RICH MAN DID NOT COMPLAIN THAT HIS PUNISHMENT WAS UNFAIR

One final thing needs to be addressed. We find the rich man complaining about his agonizing situation in Hades but we never find him complaining that his judgment was unfair. He realized that he received the punishment which he deserved. When all is said and done, judgment by God will always be recognized as fair.

THERE IS EVIDENCE OF CONSCIOUSNESS IN THE INTERMEDIATE STATE

If people lapse into unconsciousness after death, then there is no purpose whatsoever for this story. This account only makes sense if it gives us genuine details of what happens immediately after death.

What it does provide is a contrast of believers and unbelievers after death. It also gives us a look into the unseen world of the wicked dead. For them, their fate is truly horrific.

SUMMARY TO QUESTION 11
WHAT CAN BE LEARNED ABOUT THE AFTERLIFE FROM THE ACCOUNT OF THE RICH MAN AND LAZARUS? (LUKE 16:19-31)

The story which Jesus told about the rich man and Lazarus gives us the clearest picture in Scripture of the in-between state which occurs after someone dies but before they are raised from the dead and judged. We learn so many things about what happens to a person after they die, both the righteous and the unrighteous.

To begin with, we discover that death is not the end. Indeed, there is a conscious existence in the next world. We also learn that death has a particular destination. The rich man and Lazarus each went to an actual place. The rich man went to Hades where he was in a place of conscious torment while Lazarus was being comforted in the presence of the patriarch Abraham. In this story, Lazarus remains silent. We are, however, told that he is in a place of happiness and comfort. It is

Abraham, the one who is comforting Lazarus, which does the speaking to the rich man.

What we do know is that the rich man was fully conscious of his surroundings; he was not in a state of sleep. He was well-aware of where he was and why he was there. Furthermore, he had all his senses. This includes memory of the past. He knew his own personal identity, that of Abraham, of Lazarus, of Moses, and the fact that he had five brothers who were still living.

We also find that he was at a place of no escape and no rest. He was bound to this horrible place of punishment for his sinful ways. He was also in some type of torment. Indeed, we are told that this rich man experienced thirst and was suffering in anguish. Furthermore, while he complained about the suffering he was experiencing, he did not complain that his suffering was unfair. He realized that he received the punishment which he deserved.

However, this particular rich man had the same misconception that many people have. If only his brothers would receive a message from Lazarus returning from the dead then they would believe. Jesus rebuked this idea. Even a message from one beyond the grave will not cause people to believe if they do not wish to hear the clear teachings of the Word of God. In other words, what God has already said and had committed to writing, the Bible, is sufficient for belief.

These are some of the many things we learn about the unseen realm of the dead. For the righteous it is a wonderful state of bliss but for the unrighteous it is indescribable misery.

What Are Some Questionable Conclusions That People Draw From The Story Of The Rich Man And Lazarus?

The story of the rich man and Lazarus tell us a number of things about the afterlife. We learn that the dead do not go out of existence. Indeed, all of us go to one of two destinations. The righteous, those who have believed in Jesus Christ, are with the Lord while the unrighteous are sent away from His wonderful presence. The righteous are comforted while the unrighteous are tormented. These are a few of the many things which we learn from this account.

However there are a couple of conclusions that people draw from this account that are somewhat questionable. They include the following.

1. THE DEAD HAVE ACTUAL BODIES

The story may tell us something of the bodies of both the righteous and unrighteous dead. The rich man wanted Lazarus to use his finger to give him water so that he could dip it on his tongue. The Bible puts it this way.

> 'Father Abraham!' he called out, 'Have mercy on me and send Lazarus to dip the tip of his finger in water and cool my tongue, because I am in agony in this flame!' (Luke 16:24 HCSB).

These descriptions may indicate that they both were in some type of body. In addition, the fact that he is experiencing thirst gives us the impression that he is suffering in a body.

However, this is not the only possible interpretation. There are many who believe that the suffering, while actual, is only described in terms of them having a body.

There does not seem to be enough evidence to be certain about this matter.

2. LAZARUS WAS GEOGRAPHICALLY ABOVE THE RICH MAN

It is usually thought that Lazarus was positioned geographically above the rich man. The description is as follows.

> And being in torment in Hades, he looked up and saw Abraham a long way off, with Lazarus at his side (Luke 16:23 HCSB).

Seeing Lazarus and Abraham "afar off" when he lifted up his eyes seems to indicate the rich man was below them while they were looking down at the rich man.

This is not necessarily the case. The idea of "lifting up his eyes and seeing him afar off" does not have to mean, "to look up in the sky." The direction is not what is emphasized as much as the fact that they are separated from one another.

While we can indeed draw a number of conclusions about the afterlife from Jesus' story of the rich man and Lazarus we must be careful about drawing too many conclusions from this account.

This reinforces a valuable lesson we learn from our study of Scripture. We need to discover exactly what the text says but we always need to be careful not to read more into the text than what it actually does say.

SUMMARY TO QUESTION 12
WHAT ARE SOME QUESTIONABLE CONCLUSIONS THAT PEOPLE DRAW
FROM THE STORY OF THE RICH MAN AND LAZARUS?

From the biblical story of the rich man and Lazarus we learn many things about the afterlife. The unseen realm of the dead is no longer a complete mystery.

While there are a number of things that can be learned about the afterlife from the account of the rich man and Lazarus there are some questionable conclusions that are often drawn from this account.

First, there is some question as to whether Lazarus and the rich man had actual bodies. Those who believe they had actual bodies point to the fact the story speaks of such things a finger of Lazarus, and a tongue of the rich man. The fact that the rich man could see Lazarus also seems to indicate they had bodies.

Though the impression is given that each of them had some sort of body we should not necessarily assume that this is the case. Whether or not they had actual bodies remains an open question.

Another questionable conclusion is that the righteous dead are geographically above the unrighteous dead. Indeed, it is not certain that Lazarus was geographically above the rich man though the rich man is said to have "lifted up" his eyes to see Abraham and Lazarus. The location of Lazarus with reference to the rich man is not relevant in the story except for the fact they were separated by a great chasm. The point is that there was a great divide between the righteous and the unrighteous.

Therefore, while a number conclusions can be drawn from Jesus' story of the rich man and Lazarus we need to be careful not to find more in this account than what is meant to be there.

QUESTION 13

Should The Living Attempt To
Contact The Dead? (Spiritism, Necromancy)

If the dead still exist after this life is over, then an obvious question arises: Should we who are alive attempt to contact them? Since they are on the "other side," and can tell us what it is like in the realm of the dead, should we reach out to them to discover truths we cannot know in this life? Would not our dead relatives, who are believers in Christ, help us if we contacted them? What, if anything, does the Bible have to say about this?

TALKING TO THE DEAD: SPIRITISM

Spiritism is the belief that the living can contact the dead. This is also called "necromancy." Through a person called a "medium," the living are supposedly able to speak to the spirit of a deceased person in the unseen world.

As we will discover, the Bible condemns this practice in the strongest of terms. We find the following things taught in Scripture about this subject.

1. SPIRITISM IS FORBIDDEN IN SCRIPTURE

The Bible is very clear that the living should never attempt to contact the dead. In ancient Israel those who practiced such things were put to death. Moses wrote.

> You shall not permit a female sorcerer to live (Exodus 22:18 NRSV).

The death penalty was instituted for those who practiced sorcery.

The Law also said.

> Don't eat the blood of any animal. Don't practice any kind of witchcraft ... Don't make yourselves disgusting to me by going to people who claim they can talk to the dead (Leviticus 19:26,31 CEV).

God said that He was disgusted by those who attempted to speak to the dead.

Elsewhere in Leviticus it says.

> I will be your enemy if you go to someone who claims to speak with the dead, and I will destroy you from among my people.... If you claim to receive messages from the dead, you will be put to death by stoning, just as you deserve (Leviticus 20:6,27 CEV).

This is very strong language from Scripture. God says that He will be the enemy of those who try to speak with the dead! Consequently, those who practiced such things were to be put to death in ancient Israel.

2. WE ARE NOT TO IMITATE THE HEATHEN

The people of Israel were warned, before they entered into the Promised Land, not to imitate the ways of the heathen. This includes attempting to contact the dead. Scripture gives the following warnings to the people.

> When you enter the land the LORD your God is giving you, do not learn to imitate the detestable ways of the nations there. Let no one be found among you who sacrifices his son or daughter in the fire, who practices divination or sorcery,

interprets omens, engages in witchcraft, or casts spells, or who is a medium or spiritist or who consults the dead. Anyone who does these things is detestable to the LORD, and because of these detestable practices the LORD your God will drive out those nations before you (Deuteronomy 18:9-12 NIV).

The Levitical laws forbade any attempted contact with the dead. According to the Lord, this was a detestable practice. Indeed, the Lord said that He drove the people of the other nations out of the Promised Land for doing such things.

3. THE PROPHETS SPOKE OUT AGAINST SPIRITISM

The biblical prophets also spoke out against such practices. Isaiah wrote the following condemning words against mediums.

So why are you trying to find out the future by consulting mediums and psychics? Do not listen to their whisperings and mutterings. Can the living find out the future from the dead? Why not ask your God? "Check their predictions against my testimony," says the LORD. "If their predictions are different from mine, it is because there is no light or truth in them" (Isaiah 8:19,20 NLT).

God's spokesmen made it clear that spiritism, trying to contact the dead through a medium, should not be practiced by those who follow the Lord.

Note also that the Lord says that their predictions will be *different* than His. In other words, any so-called contact with the spirits of the dead will result in them NOT telling the truth. Simply stated, they will lie.

The Lord also warned the people through the prophet Jeremiah about this detestable practice. He said.

So do not listen to your prophets, your diviners, your interpreters of dreams, your mediums or your sorcerers who tell you,

'You will not serve the king of Babylon.' They prophesy lies to you that will only serve to remove you far from your lands; I will banish you and you will perish (Jeremiah 27:9,10 NIV).

Again, we have the warning from the Lord to His people. They are not to listen to these people because they lie to them!

4. IT IS SPEAKING TO THE WRONG SOURCE

The Bible forbids talking to the dead, not because it is necessarily a hoax on the part of the medium. Rather it is because humans are attempting to receive supernatural guidance from a source other the God. Whatever the ultimate source of their information may be, whether an evil spirit or a medium who is perpetrating a hoax, the end result is always the same; people will be led away from the living God. Indeed, their behavior after the encounter will be anything but godly.

For example, in Second Chronicles we read of the detestable practices of the evil King Manasseh. Scripture says the following.

> He sacrificed his sons in the fire in the Valley of Ben Hinnom, practiced sorcery, divination and witchcraft, and consulted mediums and spiritists. He did much evil in the eyes of the LORD, provoking him to anger (2 Chronicles 33:6 NIV).

Again, we find spiritism linked with all sorts of evil. The two go hand in hand. Those who attempt to speak to the dead go astray in many other ways.

ONE FINAL MATTER: IT IS NOT POSSIBLE TO CONTACT A SPECIFIC PERSON IN THE REALM OF THE DEAD

If someone does have a conversation through a medium, in an attempt to summon up a dead friend or relative, the end result will always be the same; they will NOT be speaking to the person whom they wish to speak to!

Either they are the victims of a hoax on the part of a medium or they are speaking to a lying spirit who is pretending to be the person they are seeking. Whatever the case may be, they are being lied to. In other words, it is not possible for the living to contact the dead.

Therefore, from looking at what the Bible has to say about this topic, we conclude that spiritism, the attempt of the living to contact the dead, is not something which human beings should dabble in. It only leads to destruction.

SUMMARY TO QUESTION 13
SHOULD THE LIVING ATTEMPT TO CONTACT THE DEAD? (SPIRITISM, NECROMANCY)

From Scripture we know that the deceased do not go out of existence. Indeed, their spirits are very much alive in the unseen realm of the dead. Consequently, the question arises about contacting them. Since they are in a firsthand position to tell us about present conditions in the afterlife should we attempt to contact them? Should we ask them for information that we ourselves cannot obtain here upon the earth?

The practice of attempting to contact the dead is not something new. Indeed, in biblical times, like today, there were people who attempted to contact the spirits of the dead. A person, known as a "medium" usually acts as a go-between between the spirits of the dead and those attempting to contact these spirits. Among other things, this practice is known as "spiritism" and "necromancy."

Consequently, the Bible has much to say on the matter. We find that the Scripture, in the strongest of terms, forbids consulting the spirits of the dead. In fact, the Lord told the nation Israel that the other nations were driven out of the Promised Land for engaging in such practices.

The Lord then warned the people of Israel that they were not to imitate unbelievers in doing such evil things.

It is possible to see how much the Lord detested those who practiced spiritism. Indeed, He ordered the death penalty for those who attempted to contact the spirits of the dead.

We also discover that seeking supernatural guidance from a source other than the Lord will cause the person to be led astray. Indeed, the Bible calls them "lying spirits" because they will never tell the truth to those who are asking them for guidance.

In addition, it is difficult to determine whether the person engaged in spiritism is actually speaking to an evil spirit or whether they are being deceived. Indeed, much of the phenomena of spiritism can be attributed to deception. However, whatever the ultimate source, it is not a source of truth.

In fact, a person will never actually contact the one whom they are seeking. Instead, they will be deceived by either the medium or by a "lying spirit." In other words, it is impossible for anyone to reach their deceased friend or relative who has passed on.

Thus, the Lord informs us that such information gathered from medium will be a lie. Consequently, whatever information is derived from talking to the dead will be of no value whatsoever. To the contrary, it will deceive those who are asking.

Therefore, spiritism, or attempting to talk to the dead through a medium, is something that the believer should have nothing to do with.

QUESTION 14

Did The Dead Prophet Samuel Communicate To Saul Through A Medium At En Dor?

From the Bible, we know that the dead do not go out of existence. They are still alive and conscious in the unseen realm, the netherworld. We also discovered that the Bible clearly condemns the practice of spiritism or attempting to contact the dead. This includes the righteous dead; those who have believed in the Lord.

THE ACCOUNT OF SAUL AND THE MEDIUM AT EN DOR

Although the Bible condemns spiritism, the living talking to the dead, there is an episode in Scripture that seems to give some justification to this practice. We can explain what happened as follows.

THE BIBLICAL BACKGROUND

The book of First Samuel gives us the account of the experience of King Saul with a medium at the city of En Dor. The prophet Samuel was dead, and the army of the Philistines had gathered to fight against Israel at Mount Gilboa. Seeing the vast army of the enemy, Saul became afraid. He decided to inquire of the Lord. However, God was no longer speaking to Saul because of his continual disobedience. The Bible says.

> And when Saul inquired of the LORD, the LORD did not answer him, either by dreams or by Urim or by the prophets (1 Samuel 28:6 NKJV).

The Lord was no longer answering Saul. There was no word from Him to this disobedient king.

SAUL SEEKS OUT A MEDIUM TO DISCOVER HIS FUTURE

Since God had turned His back on Saul, the king decided to resort to spiritism, talking to the dead. Saul had previously put all the mediums out of the land.

> Now Samuel was dead, and all Israel had mourned for him and buried him in his own town of Ramah. Saul had expelled the mediums and spiritists from the land (1 Samuel 28:3 NIV).

Although all the mediums and spiritists had been driven out of the land, Saul asked his servants to find a medium that he could consult about the future, seeing that God would tell him nothing. Discovering that there was a medium at the town of En Dor, Saul disguised himself to get information about the future.

SAUL CONSULTED A MEDIUM TO ASK TO SPEAK TO SAMUEL

As is fitting with the crime against the Lord he was committing, Saul came to the medium at En Dor at night. He asked her to bring up the prophet Samuel for him. The Bible says the following happened.

> When the woman saw Samuel, she screamed. Then she turned to Saul and said, "You've tricked me! You're the king!" "Don't be afraid," Saul replied. "Just tell me what you see" (1 Samuel 28:12,13 CEV).

Samuel then had a conversation with Saul.

> "Why are you bothering me by bringing me up like this?" Samuel asked. "I'm terribly worried," Saul answered. "The Philistines are about to attack me. God has turned his back on me and won't answer any more by prophets or by dreams. What should I do?" (1 Samuel 28:15 CEV).

Samuel complained to Saul about being disturbed from his place in the realm of the dead. Saul pleaded to the deceased prophet to advise him as to what to do against the armies of the Philistines.

SAMUEL PREDICTED SAUL'S DEATH

Samuel then went on to predict that Saul would die the next day.

> The Lord will deliver both Israel and you into the hands of the Philistines, and tomorrow you and your sons will be with me. The Lord will also give the army of Israel into the hands of the Philistines (1 Samuel 28:19 NIV).

The Scripture tells us that Saul did indeed die as Samuel predicted.

> When the battle intensified against Saul, the archers caught up with him and severely wounded him. Then Saul said to his armor-bearer, "Draw your sword and run me through with it, or these uncircumcised men will come and run me through and torture me." But his armor-bearer would not do it because he was terrified. Then Saul took his sword and fell on it. When his armor-bearer saw that Saul was dead, he also fell on his own sword and died with him (1 Samuel 31:3-5 HCSB).

Samuel's status as a prophet survived his death! Saul died the very next day.

THERE ARE NUMBER OF QUESTIONS TO ANSWER ABOUT THIS STORY

There are many questions that arise about this account: Who appeared to Saul? Was it the prophet Samuel? If it was not Samuel who appeared to Saul, then what happened? Was it a trick by the medium, some sort of demonic manifestation, or some hallucination by Saul?

If it was Samuel, then how was he able to appear? Did God allow him to speak to Saul, or did the medium have the power to call up the righteous dead?

These questions have been long-debated. We will examine each major option and then summarize our findings.

OPTION 1: SAMUEL DID NOT APPEAR

It is possible that Samuel did not appear to Saul. There are a number of arguments which are raised against an actual appearance of Samuel. They are as follows.

1. WHY SPEAK TO SAUL THIS WAY?

Saul had earlier attempted to inquire of the Lord but He would not speak to him through the biblically ordained means? Why then would the Lord speak to Saul through a medium at a séance? It does not seem to make sense that He would.

2. THE BIBLE CONDEMNS MEDIUMS AND THEIR WORK

As we have noted, God has always spoken against consulting mediums in the strongest of terms. Why would He act contrary to what He had previously revealed? Since God does not change, this could not have been an authentic appearance of Samuel.

3. THIS IS A STRANGE PLACE FOR A MIRACLE

This would have been a strange place for God to perform a miracle. There is no similar example in Scripture of God speaking His Word in the midst of such an obvious evil environment. This would be a unique situation.

4. THE PROPHECY DID NOT COME TO PASS

Some have argued that the prediction did not come to pass. His enemies did not kill Saul. In fact, he killed himself. Therefore the prophecy was false. Since it was a false prophecy, God could not have given it.

5. THE DEAD CANNOT RETURN

Furthermore, the Bible teaches that the dead cannot return to communicate to the living. After the death of his son, David testified that the child could not return to him.

> But now that he is dead, why should I fast? Can I bring him back again? I will go to him, but he will not return to me (2 Samuel 12:23 NIV).

Since the Bible teaches the dead cannot return, this could not have been the appearance of dead prophet Samuel.

6. THIS SEEMS TO GIVE CREDENCE FOR SPIRITISM

A final objection to the genuine appearance of Samuel is that it seems to give some sort of credence to the living talking to the dead. If God allowed it on this one occasion, then why wouldn't He do it on other occasions? This opens the door for believers to dabble into areas in which God expressly forbids them.

It is for these reasons that the idea that Samuel actually appeared to Saul at En Dor is roundly rejected by many.

WHAT DID HAPPEN?

If this is the case, then there are basically three things that could have happened when Saul met the medium. They are as follows.

POSSIBILITY 1: A DEMONIC SPIRIT SPOKE TO SAUL

It has been argued that the medium actually called up a spirit from the afterlife, but that spirit was not Samuel. It was a demon impersonating Samuel. This demon, impersonating Samuel, told Saul only part of the truth.

The Bible teaches that demons are able to utter half-truths. The Book of Acts tells us that a woman who was possessed with an evil spirit followed the Apostle Paul.

The girl followed Paul and the rest of us and kept yelling, "These men are servants of the Most High God! They are telling you how to be saved" (Acts 16:17 CEV).

Part of what she said was true. Indeed, the apostles were proclaiming the true way of salvation. However her overall message was one of deception.

RESPONSE

The text does not represent this as a demon impersonation. If it was a demonic spirit instead of Samuel, then why did this spirit tell the entire truth? There were no-half truths in the response of this personage to Saul. This is not consistent with the way demon spirits work. The message sounded like something Samuel himself would have said, if he were still alive. This is one of many signs in the account that it was an authentic appearance of Samuel.

POSSIBILITY 2: IT WAS A FAKE APPEARANCE

There is also the view that the medium faked Samuel's appearance. Saul was tricked into believing that it was really Samuel when it was only some type of deception on the part of the medium. The arguments for this are as follows:

1. THE WOMAN WAS CALLED A VENTRILOQUIST

The Septuagint, the Greek translation of the Hebrew Old Testament, uses the word *eggastrimuthos* (ventriloquist) to describe the woman (verse 9) and those who practice the same type of divination. This indicates that she had the ability to deceive people into thinking there was some other personage present by the throwing of her voice.

2. SHE PROBABLY RECOGNIZED SAUL

Though she pretended ignorance, the woman probably recognized Saul from the beginning. We should not assume that his disguise fooled her.

Indeed, the Bible makes it clear that Saul was much taller than all of the other people of Israel. Therefore, it would have been hard for him to disguise himself.

3. SAUL WAS PREVENTED FROM VIEWING SAMUEL

In addition, it was only the medium that saw Samuel. Saul did not. He was prevented from viewing the spirit. Consequently she only pretended to be surprised by the appearance of the prophet Samuel when, most likely, she saw nothing.

4. HE RELIED ON WHAT SHE SAID

Since the king saw and heard nothing, he had to rely on the woman to tell him what this spirit was saying. He did not converse directly to Samuel. Therefore, we do not really know if Samuel appeared.

5. THIS WAS NOT A GREAT PREDICTION

To say that Saul would die the next day in battle was not any great prediction seeing that they were vastly outnumbered by the Philistines.

6. SAUL KILLED HIMSELF

Finally, Saul did not die by the hand of the Philistines the next day. He killed himself after he had been wounded.

All these arguments have lead many to assume we have a hoax on the part of the woman and not a genuine appearance of Samuel.

RESPONSE

The main problem with this view is there is nothing in the account to indicate that it was a hoax. A straightforward reading causes one to assume that Samuel actually appeared.

Also, the medium herself seemed genuinely terrified when Samuel appeared. The Bible explains what happened in this manner.

> When the woman saw Samuel, she screamed, "You've deceived me! You are Saul!" "Don't be afraid!" the king told her. "What do you see?" "I see a god coming up out of the earth," she said (1 Samuel 28:12,13 NLT).

The passage does not give the impression that she was acting. The visitor was not whom she was expecting. This implies that there was some authentic appearance of the dead rather than it being her own demonic ability or trickery. She was not expecting Samuel to appear.

Also, the account does not say that it was *only* the woman who heard and saw Samuel. She saw him at the beginning and explained to Saul what he looked like. When the conversation of Samuel and Saul took place there is no indication that Samuel spoke through the woman rather than speaking directly to Saul.

POSSIBILITY 3: SAUL SUFFERED A HALLUCINATION

It is also possible that Saul had some sort of hallucination when he thought he spoke to the dead prophet Samuel. Since he desperately wanted to talk to Samuel, Saul fooled himself into believing that he was actually conversing with the dead prophet.

RESPONSE

This hallucination was not limited to Saul. The medium saw it also and was horrified. This would rule out something that was merely in the mind of Saul. The text also implies that the woman talked to Samuel. Consequently we are dealing with more than a hallucination.

SUMMARY TO OPTION 1

There are a number of reasons why the appearance of Samuel to Saul at En Dor is denied. It seems to contradict the way God works in the rest of Scripture as well as give credence to spiritism. Because of these factors, many Bible students deny that the dead prophet Samuel actually appeared to speak to Saul.

OPTION 2: SAMUEL DID APPEAR TO SAUL

There are, however, many Bible students who believe that it was actually Samuel who spoke to King Saul that night. A straightforward reading of the account makes this apparent. The reasons for holding this view are as follows.

1. THE BIBLE SAYS SAMUEL APPEARED

The Bible says Samuel appeared (verses 12,14,15,16,20). This seems to settle the matter as to the identity of the spirit that spoke to Saul. The text is very explicit. It was actually Samuel that spoke to the wayward king.

2. THE DESCRIPTION OF SAMUEL IS CORRECT

The description of Samuel is authentic. The medium said that Samuel was wearing a robe of a prophet. This was the robe Saul had taken and ripped as Samuel declared the kingdom had been ripped out of his hand. We read about this earlier in Samuel.

> Now therefore, please forgive my sin and return with me so I can worship the LORD. Samuel replied to Saul, "I will not return with you. Because you rejected the word of the LORD, the LORD has rejected you from being king over Israel." When Samuel turned to go, Saul grabbed the hem of his robe, and it tore (1 Samuel 15:27-28 HCSB).

This would have convinced Saul that it was actually Samuel.

3. THE REACTION OF THE MEDIUM

The medium reacted as though the spirit of Samuel actually appeared. She was terrified and cried out and the top of her voice. Her reaction suggests that his appearance was unexpected. This was something different than what usually happened when she practiced her occultic art.

She claimed she saw a god (Hebrew *Elohim*). This probably refers to the spirit of one who had died. This is an indication that she was not really expecting the genuine spirit of Samuel to appear. Whatever she had expected to happen was thwarted by Samuel's actual appearance.

4. THE PRIOR EXCHANGE BETWEEN SAUL AND SAMUEL

The words of Samuel to Saul alluded to a prior conversation between the two. Only the real Samuel would have said this to Saul, not some impersonator. This is another indication that Samuel truly appeared.

5. SAMUEL WAS A PROPHET

Samuel's role as a prophet in Scripture is well-documented. The message he gave Saul with respect to his future is consistent with what we know about Samuel and his office as a prophet.

6. HIS PREDICTION WAS CORRECT

Samuel said that Saul would join him the next day in the realm of the dead. Saul did die the next day. Consequently, the prediction was correct. Since only God knows the future, it must have been Samuel who spoke to Saul. It is not a contradiction that Saul fell upon his sword and killed himself. He was in the process of dying when he took his own life.

7. IT IS ANOTHER UNUSUAL METHOD OF COMMUNICATION BY GOD

While God did use an unusual method of communicating His Word, this was not the first time He has done something like this. Indeed, God also used an unusual method in communicating His message to Balaam (Numbers 22). He spoke through a donkey. Therefore, we should not limit God's methods in speaking to humanity.

8. SAUL BOWED TO SAMUEL

The fact that Saul bowed in obeisance to Samuel showed that he understood it was really Samuel who had appeared. It is clear that Saul knew that he had been talking to Samuel.

9. THE MESSAGE IS CONSISTENT WITH THE REST OF SCRIPTURE

The message given was consistent with something God or Samuel might have said. There is nothing inconsistent in this message with respect to God's nature or His plan for humanity. In other words, the message from Samuel did not contradict anything else revealed in Scripture.

10. THE READING OF THE SEPTUAGINT

The Septuagint, the Greek translation of the Hebrew Old Testament, adds these words after 1 Chronicles 10:13,14.

Saul asked counsel of her that had a familiar spirit to inquire of her, and Samuel made answer to him.

This addition to the text, gives further testimony to the belief that it was actually Samuel who appeared.

HOW DID IT HAPPEN?

If it was Samuel who appeared to Saul, then there are two basic possibilities as to how he appeared. Either the medium actually called up Samuel by demonic power, or Samuel appeared by God's design. From Scripture, we can say the following about these possibilities.

POSSIBILITY 1: DID THE MEDIUM CALL UP SAMUEL?

It has been argued that the medium, through demonic power, actually called up Samuel from the realm of the dead. This would have been a demonic miracle. The Bible warns us about the power of the devil. Paul wrote about the lying wonders he will make.

> The coming of the lawless one will be in accordance with the work of Satan displayed in all kinds of counterfeit miracles, signs and wonders, and in every sort of evil that deceives those who are perishing. They perish because they refused to love the truth and so be saved (2 Thessalonians 2:9,10 NIV).

Satan can perform signs which deceive.

Jesus said there were those people who falsely spoke in His name. We read Him saying the following.

> On judgment day many will tell me, 'Lord, Lord, we prophesied in your name and cast out demons in your name and performed many miracles in your name' (Matthew 7:22 NLT).

Some believe that the devil has such power.

RESPONSE

Though Satan and his demons can perform deceiving signs, they are always under God's ultimate control. God is the only One who has the authority over life and death. Satan has no such power or authority.

SATAN CANNOT DO MIRACLES

In addition, there is no evidence that Satan, or his demons, can perform actual miracles. Therefore, the miracle of calling the spirit of Samuel from the realm of the righteous dead is not something that Satan, or his demons, have the power to do. Those who are in God's hands are protected from Satan's power.

TALKING TO THE DEAD IS CONDEMNED

Finally, we see that attempting to contact the dead through a medium is actually condemned in this passage. Samuel said to Saul.

> Samuel said, "Why do you consult me, now that the LORD has turned away from you and become your enemy?" (1 Samuel 28:16 NIV).

Saul was rebuked for consulting the medium. All of these factors would indicate that Samuel was not called up by some demonic power.

POSSIBILITY 2: DID SAMUEL APPEAR BY GOD'S POWER?

Since it seems that Samuel did appear, and that it was not due to demonic intervention, the best answer seems to be that Samuel was permitted to appear by God's power. On this one occasion, God allowed Samuel to be brought from His presence to speak to Saul. It was His final word of judgment to the disobedient king.

THIS IS NOT A BASIS FOR TALKING TO MEDIUMS

Whatever happened in this episode, it is not to be used as a basis of attempting to contact the dead through mediums. In the strongest of terms, God forbids any contact with those who attempt to reach out to the deceased. The result of what happened to King Saul, his death the next day after he consulted a medium, serves as a further warning not to delve into this forbidden area. We read in Chronicles.

> So Saul died for his breach of faith. He broke faith with the Lord in that he did not keep the command of the Lord, and also consulted a medium, seeking guidance. He did not seek guidance from the Lord. Therefore the Lord put him to death and turned the kingdom over to David the son of Jesse (1 Chronicles 10:13,14 ESV).

The Bible gives no encouragement whatsoever about consulting mediums. None!

THERE IS SURVIVAL BEYOND GRAVE

This episode does establish that, at this time in Israel's history, there was a belief that there was life beyond the grave. In that life, people kept their personal identity. Samuel appeared in the same form in which he had died; as an old man wearing a robe.

Obviously this is a fascinating episode in the history of Israel. While many of the questions about this account are debated, it seems that we can come away with a number of definite conclusions.

SUMMARY TO QUESTION 14
DID THE DEAD PROPHET SAMUEL COMMUNICATE TO SAUL THROUGH A MEDIUM AT EN DOR?

The Bible says that at the city of En Dor in ancient Israel an episode occurred between King Saul and a woman who was a medium, one who contacted the dead. The Bible says that upon the request of Saul, she called up the spirit of the dead prophet Samuel. Samuel appeared and spoke to Saul about his upcoming death the next day in battle with the Philistines. The fact is that Saul did die the next day.

It has been long-debated as to whether it was really Samuel who spoke to Saul rather than some demonic spirit, or some trick on behalf of the medium. The best evidence seems to lead us to believe that it was actually Samuel who appeared. Indeed, Scripture specifically says five times that it was Samuel who spoke to Saul.

If it was the prophet Samuel, there is also the question of why and how he was allowed to appear. Scripture is silent as to why Samuel was allowed to speak to Saul from the next world; something which the Lord clearly prohibited the people of Israel to do.

Furthermore, why would God speak at all to Saul after earlier refusing to talk to the wayward king? Indeed, these are some of the many unanswered questions that surround this episode.

Whatever the case may be, this story does not give any basis for the living to attempt to contact the dead. In fact, the fate of Saul gives further testimony of the bad things that happen when people attempt to contact those in the spirit world rather than reaching out to the true and living God.

QUESTION 15

What Is The Doctrine Of Purgatory?

The biblical position is that all those who die will spend eternity in heaven or hell. Before we reach our final destination, everyone is in a state of conscious existence after death. Believers are in the presence of the Lord while unbelievers are not.

Death closes the period of probation that all of us have here on earth. What is done in this life will determine where we spend the next. After death, comes the judgment. The Bible teaches this. We read the following in the Book of Hebrews.

> And just as it is destined that each person dies only once and after that comes judgment (Hebrews 9:27 NLT).

Although this is the biblical teaching, certain unbiblical views of the intermediate state have arisen. One of them is the doctrine of purgatory. This is held by the Roman Catholic Church and the Orthodox Church. We can sum up this belief as follows.

1. BELIEVERS DO NOT GO STRAIGHT TO HEAVEN

Those who believe in purgatory teach that not every believer who dies goes immediately to heaven. Even if a person dies at peace with the church, if they are not perfect, they have to go through a time of purging. The only people who enter heaven immediately are some martyrs, and other highly favored individuals. Most people still need to be refined or purified before entering God's presence.

Thus, they go to this place of purging called purgatory. All unbaptized adults, and those Christians who have committed mortal sins after baptism, go immediately to hell. However, most Christians who are not good enough to go straight to heaven must go to purgatory. In other words, heaven is delayed at death.

2. THERE IS A PLACE OF PURGING

Purgatory can be defined as a temporary place, or state, where the souls of most believers go after death. It is an intermediate state for the believing dead.

Although these people have been forgiven of their sins, they are still liable to experience some temporary punishment before their admittance to heaven. This is because nothing that is defiled can enter into God's presence. Because they must be properly freed from the blemish of some defects they had received after baptism, they have to work out their salvation in purgatory through suffering and a process of purification in this place which is located somewhere between earth and heaven.

THE BACKGROUND OF THE BELIEF

Some early Christians taught that when the believer died they went to a place that was a little superior to earthly existence. In this place, they had to wait for the resurrection. While waiting they had to become prepared for heaven. This involved the purging of sin. Consequently many elaborate teachings arose that were connected with this place of waiting, purgatory.

THE NEED FOR PURGATORY

The doctrine of purgatory supposes that some people die with smaller faults for which there was no true repentance. The temporal penalty of sin is, at times, not entirely paid for in this life. Since only perfect people may enter heaven, they need to be perfected of their sins.

Roman Catholics, as well as those of the Orthodox Church, have reached the conclusion that there must be a purgatory out of which people can be prayed, and released from these imperfections. Suffering for a shorter or longer time is based upon the degree of their guilt.

IT HAS NOTHING TO DO WITH SALVATION

The works done in purgatory have nothing to do with salvation. The process of purgatory is a negative one. It is a purification of those blemishes that remain after a person dies. Since death ends all opportunity for good works, the removal of defects can only occur by means of passive punishment, not good deeds done by that person. The sufferings in purgatory are both punitive and refining. They punish the believer for their sins as well as prepare them for heaven.

THERE ARE VENIAL AND MORTAL SINS

Roman Catholicism makes a distinction between venial and mortal sins. According to Roman Catholic theology, if a Roman Catholic dies in the state of mortal sin, they forfeit their chance even for purgatory. Unbaptized adults and those who have committed mortal sins after baptism go straight to hell. There is no purgatory for them. If a person commits a mortal sin they can be restored through the sacrament of Penance. However, without penance they will be sent to hell.

VENIAL SINS CAN BE FORGIVEN

Venial sins do not cause eternal damnation. They are sins which can be forgiven. Yet if a person dies with an unpaid debt for venial sins, then they must spend time in purgatory. There are, however, disagreements as to which sins are venial and which are mortal. There has been no authoritative list to separate the two.

THE NATURE OF PUNISHMENT IS DEBATED

In addition, there is no agreement as to the nature of the punishment in purgatory. Some Roman Catholic writers teach that punishment is horrible, lasting thousands of years, while others see little punishment or no punishment whatsoever.

A PERSON CAN HAVE THEIR TIME IN PURGATORY SHORTENED

There are a number of ways in which venial or smaller sins can be forgiven and the time in purgatory shortened. They are as follows.

1. GIFTS OR SERVICES RENDERED FOR THE CHURCH BY THE LIVING

The living can actually help those in purgatory. They can provide gifts to the church as well as do services on behalf of the dead person. This will supposedly shorten their time in purgatory.

The living can purchase an "indulgence" on behalf of the dead. An indulgence is a certificate which is already signed by the pope which pardons sin. It may forgive all or part of the temporal punishment for sin.

This has been one of the main ways in which the Roman Catholic Church has raised money. Historically, these indulgences were first sold to the living. These people needed a particular sin to be forgiven so as to grant them access to heaven. Later, indulgences were sold to relatives on behalf of their dead loved ones who were in purgatory. Purchasing these indulgences would lessen their suffering.

It is believed that the pope on earth has been given the authority to determine the length of ones stay in purgatory. Therefore, his authority not only extends to the church on the earth but also to believers who have not made it into heaven. Hence, it is believed that he has some jurisdiction over who is forgiven of their sin and who can enter heaven at a particular time.

Those who bought the indulgences were seen as performing a "Christian" act. This would elevate their own status before the Lord and thus, lessen their own suffering in purgatory. Consequently, they can lessen their suffering before they get to purgatory with Christian acts performed here upon the earth.

2. PRAYERS BY PRIESTS CAN RELIEVE THE SUFFERING

The prayers of priests are another way in which the sufferer in purgatory can have his or her time shortened. It is believed that their prayers have special merit for the dead. Therefore, priestly prayers can influence what happens in the realm of the believing dead who have not reached heaven.

3. MASSES PROVIDED BY RELATIVES

Relatives and friends of the deceased can have masses done on their behalf. This is another way in which the sufferer's time can be shortened.

All of these are supposedly able to shorten the time and suffering in purgatory for that particular person.

THERE WILL BE AN END OF PURGATORY

The suffering in purgatory is not endless. All suffering of believers will end at the Last Judgment. At that time, purgatory will cease to exist.

WHERE IS PURGATORY?

Purgatory supposedly exists but there does not seem to be any consensus as to where exactly it is located. In one sense, it is a place somewhere between earth and heaven; a halfway house between this world and our ultimate destination with Christ. However, to locate it geographically does not seem to be possible since it exists in the unseen realm.

This briefly sums up the doctrine of purgatory as it is generally taught.

THE DOCTRINE OF PURGATORY CONTRADICTS SCRIPTURE

However, as we will see, this idea is contrary to a number of doctrines of the Christian faith including the biblical doctrine of salvation from sin. Our next three questions examine the doctrine of purgatory in some detail.

SUMMARY TO QUESTION 15
WHAT IS THE DOCTRINE OF PURGATORY?

The Roman Catholic Church and the Orthodox Church do not believe that most Christians will enter heaven immediately upon their death. Instead, there is an intermediate place where they must first go to have their sins purged. This place, which exists between heaven and earth, is called purgatory. Since a person may still have some sins that have not been paid for in this life, they must go to purgatory where their sins are purged. Once the sins have been sufficiently purged, that person can then enter the perfection of heaven.

The Roman Catholic Church teaches that the suffering in purgatory is proportionate to the sins committed in this life. The time spent can vary from a relatively short period, such as a few hours, to thousands of years. However, there is no consensus of opinion as to the duration of the stay in purgatory, or the type of punishment one receives. No one seems to be able to give any authoritative answer to this question. Unbaptized adults and those who have committed a mortal sin after baptism go directly to hell. Purgatory is only for believers.

While Christians must spend time in purgatory, it supposedly can be lessened by a number of things. The living can do services and give gifts to the church to shorten the time of their loved one. This includes purchasing indulgences or certificates signed by the pope which can forgive sin. This indicates that the pope on earth has some jurisdiction in the next world.

Prayers by priests as well as having masses in the name of the dead can also shorten the time a person spends in purgatory. The dead can do nothing in purgatory to help themselves. It is only their living friends and loved ones who can help them. They are completely dependent upon them to shorten their stay in this place of purging.

Purgatory is only a temporary place. It will end when the Last Judgment occurs. Like death and Hades it will be thrown into the lake of fire.

From that time forward, no more suffering will be necessary because everyone will be perfected, ready to enter heaven.

This sums up the doctrine of purgatory. A close inspection of Scripture will find that purgatory is not a biblical doctrine but actually contradicts the Bible on a number of crucial issues.

Is There Such A Place
As Purgatory?

The doctrine of purgatory says that believers in Jesus Christ, with few exceptions, must enter into a type of purging before they enter heaven. Thus, they have to go to halfway place between earth and heaven, purgatory. This is the doctrine of the Roman Catholic Church and the Orthodox Church.

Is there such a place as purgatory? Will Christians have to further suffer for their sins once this life is over? What does the Scripture say?

THERE IS NO BIBLICAL SUPPORT FOR ITS EXISTENCE

Although the Scripture speaks of fire as purification, it knows nothing of a purifying process between death and resurrection that the believer must encounter. The idea of a purgatory has no support from Scripture. Furthermore, it contradicts the clear teaching of the Bible. We can make the following observations.

1. ALL BELIEVERS ARE IN GOD'S PRESENCE IMMEDIATELY UPON DEATH AND THEY ARE BEING COMFORTED

When the Scripture is studied there are two essential truths that contradict the idea of purgatory; the righteous dead are immediately conscious in God's presence and they are joyful. These truths are plainly stated and should be decisive in any question as to the existence of such a place of suffering.

From a study of Scripture we learn about these wonderful truths.

ALL BELIEVERS ARE IN GOD'S PRESENCE AT THE MOMENT OF DEATH

Scripture teaches that believers go immediately to the presence of the Lord upon death. Paul wrote the following to the Corinthians.

> For we know that when this earthly tent we live in is taken down—when we die and leave these bodies—we will have a home in heaven, an eternal body made for us by God himself and not by human hands. We grow weary in our present bodies, and we long for the day when we will put on our heavenly bodies like new clothing.... Yes, we are fully confident, and we would rather be away from these bodies, for then we will be at home with the Lord (2 Corinthians 5:1,2,8 NLT).

Paul said all those who die believing in Christ are immediately present with the Lord upon their death. He wrote this to the Corinthian church. These were *not* spiritually mature believers. In fact, in his first letter to this church he described them in this manner.

> Brothers, I was not able to speak to you as spiritual people but as people of the flesh, as babies in Christ. I fed you milk, not solid food, because you were not yet able to receive it. In fact, you are still not able, because you are still fleshly. For since there is envy and strife among you, are you not fleshly and living like ordinary people? (1 Corinthians 3:1-3 HCSB).

There were still a number of problems in the church when Paul wrote his second letter to these believers. Yet each and every one of these carnal Corinthians was promised that upon their death they would be with Christ; immediately present with the Lord. There is never a hint of waiting, or suffering they would have to endure for their less than perfect spiritual lifestyle. None whatsoever!

In another place, Paul wrote to the Philippians about his desire to die and be with Christ. He stated it this way.

For I am hard pressed between the two, having a desire to depart and be with Christ, *which* is far better (Philippians 1:23 NKJV).

Again we find that the believer in Jesus Christ is in God's presence immediately upon their death. Furthermore, Paul said he would be far better off to be with Christ than to remain in this body.

Why would he say this if he had the fires of purgatory to look forward to? Paul believed that he would be immediately with Jesus Christ the moment he died. This would not only be true for him it would also be the same for every Christian.

THE BELIEVING DEAD ARE IMMEDIATELY HAPPY IN GOD'S PRESENCE

The Bible also speaks of the believing dead as being immediately happy in the presence of the Lord. There are a number of examples of this which we find in God's Word. We will give two illustrations.

LAZARUS

In Jesus' story of two deceased people who were alive and conscious in the unseen realm of the dead, the rich man and Lazarus, we find that Lazarus was happy and content in the company of Abraham while the rich man was suffering in torment. The Bible explains it this way.

> The time came when the beggar died and the angels carried him to Abraham's side. The rich man also died and was buried. In Hades, where he was in torment, he looked up and saw Abraham far away, with Lazarus by his side.... Abraham replied, 'Son, remember that in your lifetime you received your good things, while Lazarus received bad things, but now he is comforted here and you are in agony (Luke 16:22,23,25 NIV).

Though the bodies of each of them were still in the grave, we find that each of them had a conscious existence after death. The existence was either one of conscious blessing or of torment. Lazarus, the believer, was comforted by Abraham. He was *not* in some place of suffering.

THE CRIMINAL WHO DIED NEXT TO JESUS

There is further evidence of this in the words of Jesus to the criminal dying next to Him on the cross. Jesus told this dying man that he would be immediately with Jesus in Paradise. Luke records the following.

> And he said to him, "Truly, I say to you, today you will be with me in Paradise (Luke 23:43 ESV).

This man was promised paradise, not purgatory. How could the dead be immediately happy in paradise if they had to go through the fires of purgatory? The doctrine of purgatory offers no comfort to the believer who is facing death.

Furthermore, since this man was crucified for being a criminal, it is obvious that he would not be in any spiritual state to enter heaven if it was dependent upon his good deeds. Indeed, he didn't have any good deeds!

SCRIPTURE SAYS WE ARE WELCOMED TO HEAVEN

We also discover that Scripture says that all believers will be welcomed into heaven. Peter wrote about this.

> Therefore, my brothers and sisters, make every effort to confirm your calling and election. For if you do these things, you will never stumble, and you will receive a rich welcome into the eternal kingdom of our Lord and Savior Jesus Christ. (2 Peter 1:10,11 NIV).

This welcome is in contrast to the doctrine of purgatory which is anything but a welcoming thing for which to look forward.

2. THE CHURCH HAS NO AUTHORITY TO FORGIVE SIN

There is another important point we must emphasize. The church upon the earth does not have any authority to forgive sins, either by prayers, or the sacrifice of the Mass. Only God can forgive sin. The Lord has said.

> I—yes, I alone—am the one who blots out your sins for my own sake and will never think of them again (Isaiah 43:25 NLT).

Forgiveness of sin is something which belongs to God alone. We have no authority to do it.

The church may declare someone forgiven, if they have met the proper conditions that God sets down; faith in Jesus Christ. After His resurrection, Jesus said to His disciples that they had authority to declare to someone that their sins were forgiven. John records.

> Then he breathed on them and said, "Receive the Holy Spirit. If you forgive anyone's sins, they will be forgiven. But if you don't forgive their sins, they will not be forgiven" (John 20:22,23 CEV).

However, the church has no power, in and of themselves, to remove the consequences of sin, either in this world, or in the next. We can merely assure people their sins have been forgiven if they place their faith in Jesus Christ. That is all that Christians are able to do, nothing else.

Indeed, God is the only one who can forgive, and who has the power to judge. The doctrine of purgatory removes this from His hand.

3. CHRIST'S SACRIFICE WAS COMPLETE

Furthermore, the death of Jesus Christ on the cross was sufficient to pay the entire penalty for our sins. Nothing else is needed. There are a number of important points about this truth which we need to make.

JESUS DID EVERYTHING NECESSARY

Jesus made the claim that He did everything necessary to secure our salvation. John records Him praying the following to God the Father.

I brought glory to you here on earth by doing everything you told me to do (John 17:4 NLT).

Jesus has done everything necessary. Everything.

Jesus Last Words Were "It Is Finished"

When He died upon the cross, Jesus acknowledged that He has finished the task which God the Father had given to Him.

When Jesus had received the sour wine, He said, "It is finished!" Then bowing His head, He gave up His spirit (John 19:30 HCSB).

Salvation from sin is now possible because Jesus finished the work necessary to secure it for us. He has completed everything which was required.

HIS ONE SACRIFICE WAS SUFFICIENT

The writer to the Hebrews makes it clear that the *one* sacrifice of Christ on the cross was sufficient to pay for our sins. He wrote.

So also Christ died only once as a sacrifice to take away the sins of many people. He will come again but not to deal with our sins again. This time he will bring salvation to all those who are eagerly waiting for him (Hebrews 9:28 NLT).

This is a past act, never again to be repeated.

OUR SINS HAVE ALREADY BEEN PURGED

Purification of our sins has been paid in full by Jesus Christ. The Bible says.

He is the reflection of God's glory and the exact imprint of God's very being, and he sustains all things by his powerful word. When he had made purification for sins, he sat down at the right hand of the Majesty on high (Hebrews 1:3 NRSV).

Jesus paid it all, so we do not have to suffer. We cannot add to what he has done. He has done it all for us.

JESUS WAS NOT LIKE THE EARTHLY PRIESTS

We again read in Hebrews about the once-and-for-all sacrifice of Jesus Christ where the writer compares the one sacrifice of Christ to the yearly sacrifices made by the various High Priests. He explained the difference that Jesus makes.

> If he had offered himself every year, he would have suffered many times since the creation of the world. But instead, near the end of time he offered himself once and for all, so that he could be a sacrifice that does away with sin (Hebrews 9:26 CEV).

This was a one-time event. It took care of sin once-and-for-all.

WE HAVE BEEN PERFECTED FOREVER

Furthermore, those who believe in Jesus Christ are perfected forever. Again, we read in the Book of Hebrews.

> For by one offering He has perfected forever those who are being sanctified (Hebrews 10:14 NKJV).

No more sacrifices are necessary. Scripture could not be clearer on this point. We cannot improve on what Jesus Christ has done for us. Unhappily, the doctrine of purgatory says we can.

4. CHRIST CLEANSES US FROM ALL SIN

It is the blood of Jesus Christ that cleanses us from all sin, not our own suffering. John wrote the following.

> But if we are living in the light of God's presence, just as Christ is, then we have fellowship with each other, and the blood of Jesus, his Son, cleanses us from every sin. If we say

we have no sin, we are only fooling ourselves and refusing to accept the truth. But if we confess our sins to him, he is faithful and just to forgive us and to cleanse us from every wrong (1 John 1:7-9 NLT).

John says that each and every sin has been forgiven because of Jesus Christ and His death on the cross. What this means is, if the doctrine of purgatory is true, then either the suffering for sin offered by Christ was insufficient, or God the Father is exacting further punishment from believers even though the penalty for sin has already been paid. Both of these concepts are contrary to the clear teaching of Scripture.

However, there is no necessity for His sacrifice to continue. His offering on the cross means nothing else is necessary. As we have just noted, the writer to the Hebrews stated it in this manner.

> For by one offering He has perfected forever those who are sanctified (Hebrews 10:14 HCSB).

The Contemporary English Version put it this way.

> By his one sacrifice he has forever set free from sin the people he brings to God (Hebrews 10:14 CEV).

His offering perfected us for all time. We are ready for heaven the moment we believe in Jesus Christ because we have been credited with His righteousness. Nothing else is necessary.

Obviously, we do not become experientially perfect the moment we trust Christ. Indeed, we still commit sins. This is evident to everyone. But we do become positionally perfect because we are "in Christ."

5. WE TRADE OUR SIN FOR HIS RIGHTEOUSNESS

This brings us to our next point. We are credited with the righteousness of Jesus Christ the moment we believe in Him. The Bible says that Jesus took the penalty for our sin upon Himself and consequently we receive His righteousness. Paul wrote the following to the Corinthians.

He made the One who did not know sin to be sin for us,
so that we might become the righteousness of God in Him
(2 Corinthians 5:21 HCSB).

We trade our sins for His righteousness! This is the wonderful offer that
Christ makes to each and every one of us.

6. WE ARE JUSTIFIED BY FAITH ALONE

How do we receive this righteousness of Jesus Christ? Paul made it clear
that the righteousness of Christ is credited to those who simply believe
in Jesus. In other words, it is not by our works. He wrote to the Romans.

However, to the man who does not work but trusts God
who justifies the wicked, his faith is credited as righteousness
(Romans 4:5 NIV).

The Bible emphasizes that a person is made right with God by faith
alone. Good works do not enter into the process. Paul wrote.

For we hold that a person is justified by faith apart from
works prescribed by the law (Romans 3:28 NRSV).

Works cannot save a person; only Jesus Christ can save.

Salvation is a gift of God, not something we can earn through our good
deeds. Paul wrote to the Ephesians.

For by grace you have been saved through faith, and this is
not your own doing; it is the gift of God—not the result of
works, so that no one may boast (Ephesians 2:8,9 NRSV).

Here Paul specifically said that our salvation is not by means of our
works. Consequently, there is nothing which we can boast or brag about.

When he wrote to Titus, the Apostle Paul declared that righteousness
does not come from our own works. He said.

He saved us, not because of the good things we did, but because of his mercy. He washed away our sins and gave us a new life through the Holy Spirit (Titus 3:5 NLT).

It is not by works that we are justified but rather by faith and faith alone. We can do absolutely nothing to earn this salvation. We can only receive it by believing in Christ. The doctrine of purgatory assumes that good works can make a person righteous. This contradicts the biblical message of salvation.

7. THERE IS NO CONDEMNATION FOR THOSE IN CHRIST

Because of what Christ had done on behalf of believers, there is no condemnation. Paul wrote to the Romans.

Therefore, there is now no condemnation for those who are in Christ Jesus (Romans 8:1 NIV).

No condemnation means *none*. Not here or in some imaginary place like purgatory.

8. OUR CITIZENSHIP IS IN HEAVEN

There is something else which the Bible emphasizes. We are presently citizens of heaven! Our citizenship will not occur at some later time. Paul wrote.

But our citizenship is in heaven. And we eagerly await a Savior from there, the Lord Jesus Christ, who, by the power that enables him to bring everything under his control, will transform our lowly bodies so that they will be like his glorious body (Philippians 3:20-21 NIV).

Citizens of heaven will go directly to the place of blessing upon death. They will not go to some place of torment for some undetermined amount of time. According to Scripture, purgatory does not exist. Believers will not have to suffer any punishment for sins. Indeed, Jesus Christ saw to that!

9. THOSE IN THIS LIFE CANNOT CHANGE THEIR STATUS IN THE NEXT

There is also the problem of assuming that our status after death can be changed by others. The Bible is clear on this matter. It is not possible that our status be changed by deeds done by others on our behalf. It is the decisions that *we* make in this life, and this life alone, that determines our status in the next life. Others have no ability to intercede for us and change that status.

OTHER PROBLEMS WITH PURGATORY

These are only some of the problems connected with believing in a place called purgatory. We could add others.

WHY NO SPECIFIC MENTION OF IT IN SCRIPTURE?

If there is a place of purging, purgatory, where almost every Christian will go immediately upon death, then seemingly it would be essential that Christians be informed about it. Yet as we search the Scripture we find nothing directly taught about purgatory. Why? Why isn't there any specific reference to it in Scripture? Why do not we have the slightest teaching on the subject? Especially since we have many things told to us about the intermediate state. In fact, we know many things about what happens to us immediately upon death but there is nothing said about a place of purging.

This is particularly true in the Book of Revelation. With its emphasis on only "pure" people entering into heaven one would think that if purgatory existed there would at least be some reference to it. But there is none. However, no answer needs to be given because there is no such place as purgatory. On this subject the Bible is very clear!

In point of fact, the only teaching we find of a purgatory is from people living long after the time of Christ. We do not find it from Christ or His apostles.

Basically, we have to choose between the authority of God's Word, which does not teach of any such place as purgatory, and the beliefs and teachings of human beings who were not directly inspired by God.

In sum, it does not matter what some particular saint in the history of the church may have said about purgatory. What is important is what the Word of God has said. It is our only standard of authority.

Therefore, for the Bible-believer, the choice is clear. If someone cannot make a case for purgatory from the Scripture, then no case whatsoever can be made. The fact that there is complete silence in the Bible as to the existence of such a place, as well as the direct teaching in the Bible that contradicts such a doctrine, makes it plain what the Christian should believe. There is no such place as purgatory. End of story.

THERE IS NO ASSURANCE OF SALVATION WITH PURGATORY

One of the many negative by-products of a belief in purgatory is that we can never have assurance about our eternal salvation in this life. Purgatory goes hand in hand with the Roman Catholic doctrine of salvation. Salvation in Roman Catholic theology is a process; a process of becoming purified or sanctified. Since we are all "in process" we cannot be certain as to how far along we are in the process. This is in contrast to the direct teaching of the word of God which unequivocally states that we can have assurance. John wrote.

> The one who has the Son has life. The one who doesn't have the Son of God does not have life. have written these things to you who believe in the name of the Son of God, so that you may know that you have eternal life (1 John 5:12-13 HCSB).

Which is it? Can we be certain or can we not? The Bible says that we can.

PURGATORY GIVES US THE WRONG FOCUS

This brings up a further problem with holding to the doctrine of purgatory. The emphasis is not on Jesus Christ but rather upon us. This is the wrong focus! Our eyes are always to be upon who He is, not upon who we are. The writer to the Hebrews emphasized where our focus ought to be.

> Therefore, since we are surrounded by such a great cloud of witnesses, let us throw off everything that hinders and the sin that so easily entangles, and let us run with perseverance the race marked out for us. Let us fix our eyes on Jesus, the author and perfecter of our faith, who for the joy set before him endured the cross, scorning its shame, and sat down at the right hand of the throne of God (Hebrews 12:1-2 NIV).

We are to fix our eyes upon Jesus. Unhappily, the doctrine of purgatory takes the focus off of Jesus and puts it onto self.

WHAT HAPPENS TO THOSE WHO DIE BEFORE THE FINAL JUDGMENT?

There are further problems. For example, purgatory supposedly ends at the Great White Throne Judgment. But what happens to those who die immediately before this final judgment and have not been purged of their impurity? On what basis will they be allowed to enter heaven? No answer can be given.

WHERE IS PURGATORY?

While the Roman Catholic Church and the Orthodox Church sees purgatory in the future for most believers, Protestants see it in the past. Thus, we can answer the question as to the exact location of purgatory: it was on a cross two thousand years ago! This is where all our sins have been purged! And they have been purged once and for all time.

SUMMARY TO QUESTION 16
IS THERE SUCH A PLACE AS PURGATORY?

Purgatory is supposedly a place which exists somewhere between earth and heaven where the righteous are purged of any sins which have not been paid for. Once these smaller or venial sins have received the proper payment, then the person can enter heaven. This is the claim of the Roman Catholic Church and the Orthodox Church but there is absolutely no biblical basis for belief in a purgatory. Indeed, no one who has believed in Jesus Christ will have to spend even one second suffering for his or her sins in some intermediate place between earth and heaven. This can be seen as follows.

First, purgatory has no support whatsoever from Scripture. No such belief is taught or even hinted at. If the Bible is our final authority on all matters of belief and practice, then the fact that the doctrine of purgatory is absent reveals that no such place exists.

There is also the problem of making the church having any say in this matter. The church, in and of itself, has no authority to forgive sin. Only God has the ability to forgive sin. This includes the bishop of Rome, the pope. He has no authority whatsoever as to who will enter heaven after they leave this earth. None!

The idea of purgatory negates the promises of God that the believer can look forward to being in His joyous presence immediately upon death. Rather they have to look forward to a judgment by fire of undetermined length and character. This contradicts direct statements of Scripture that the believers are immediately with Him.

The idea of making a distinction between venial and mortal sins cannot be justified biblically. Sin is sin and once it is forgiven by Christ all of it has been forgiven. The Bible is clear that Christ has already purged our sins. This was a one-time event that happened in the past. The sacrifice of Jesus Christ on Calvary's cross was complete. There is nothing that we can add to it. It is Christ who cleanses us from our sin, not our own suffering.

Furthermore, being made right with God is something that happens by faith alone. Works do not enter into the picture at all. To be forgiven of our sins consists of trusting Christ, nothing more. We cannot add to what He has done for us.

These are some of the main problems with the idea of purgatory. However, there are other problems. For one thing, if purgatory is such an important doctrine then why don't we find anything about it in Scripture? One would think such an essential truth would be highlighted in the Bible. But we find nothing whatsoever.

In addition, purgatory robs the believer of any assurance of salvation. Since salvation is looked at as a process, rather than a past completed act, believers can never be assured that they have been completely saved from their sins. Neither can they know how much time they have to be purged before entering heaven. It would seem to give a very uneasy feeling for those who believe purgatory lies ahead. There is really no assurance about anything.

There are also unanswered questions with respect to purgatory such as what happens to those who die immediately before the final judgment? Seemingly, they do not have time to be purged from their imperfections to allow them to enter into heaven. What's going to happen to them? We could add many more questions such as this for which the doctrine of purgatory has no answer.

Finally, contrary to the Roman Catholic Church, purgatory is not in the future for each believer. Indeed, not only is purgatory in the past, it can be located. Purgation of all sins, past, present and future occurred two thousand years ago on a cross in the city of Jerusalem.

In sum, the doctrine of purgatory is completely at odds with what Scripture teaches on a number of essential topics. Consequently, it should be soundly rejected by Bible-believing Christians.

Is There Any Biblical Support
For Purgatory?

The Roman Catholic Church and the Orthodox Church teach that most believers will not immediately enter heaven upon death but rather go to a place of purging, or purgatory, for an undetermined amount of time. After they have been sufficiently purged they will then be allowed to enter the presence of God.

While this is the teaching about purgatory, it is not a biblical teaching. Indeed, purgatory is a belief that contradicts the clear teaching of Scripture with respect to the person and work of Jesus Christ. This, however, has not stopped people from attempting to find some biblical support for this non-biblical doctrine. The following passages are offered for the support of purgatory.

1. ISAIAH 4:4

In the Book of Isaiah there is a passage that has been used to support the doctrine of purgatory. It reads as follows.

> When the Lord has washed away the filth of the daughters of Zion and cleansed the bloodguilt from the heart of Jerusalem by a spirit of judgment and a spirit of burning (Isaiah 4:4 HCSB).

It is argued that burning, in this context, refers to the fires of judgment; a hint of the doctrine of purgatory.

2. MATTHEW 5:25,26

Jesus made a statement that is recorded in Matthew's gospel that has been used by some to argue for the doctrine of purgatory. In the Sermon on the Mount, He said the following.

> When you are on the way to court with your adversary, settle your differences quickly. Otherwise, your accuser may hand you over to the judge, who will hand you over to an officer, and you will be thrown into prison. And if that happens, you surely won't be free again until you have paid the last penny (Matthew 5:25-26 NIV).

Some Roman Catholics teach that prison is purgatory, and the last penny refers to the complete payment for the purgation of sins.

3. MATTHEW 12:32

To some, there is another statement in Matthew's gospel that seems to be speaking of purgatory. It reads as follows.

> Anyone who speaks a word against the Son of Man will be forgiven, but anyone who speaks against the Holy Spirit will not be forgiven, either in this age or in the age to come (Matthew 12:32 NIV).

It is claimed that this verse has at least an indirect reference to purgatory seeing that that Jesus left open the possibility of forgiveness in the next world.

4. MATTHEW 18:34

In this passage in Scripture Jesus talks of handing people over to the torturers until their entire debt is paid. Matthew records Him saying the following.

> And in anger his lord handed him over to be tortured until he would pay his entire debt (Matthew 18:34 NRSV).

This has been seen as a reference to the sufferings in purgatory. People will remain there and suffer torture until they pay their entire debt for the sins they have committed. They will not be able to leave until their debt is paid.

5. 1 CORINTHIANS 3:10-15

When Paul wrote to the church at Corinth, he spoke of the believer facing a coming judgment which has to do with fire. He put it this way.

> By the grace God has given me, I laid a foundation as a wise builder, and someone else is building on it. But each one should build with care. For no one can lay any foundation other than the one already laid, which is Jesus Christ. If anyone builds on this foundation using gold, silver, costly stones, wood, hay or straw, their work will be shown for what it is, because the Day will bring it to light. It will be revealed with fire, and the fire will test the quality of each person's work. If what has been built survives, the builder will receive a reward. If it is burned up, the builder will suffer loss but yet will be saved—even though only as one escaping through the flames (1 Corinthians 3:10-15 NIV).

This passage speaks of the believer being refined by fire. To some, it is a clear indication of a refining place, purgatory. Once refined, the believer can enter the presence of the Lord.

6. 2 MACCABEES 12:41-45

There is a passage in the apocryphal book of Second Maccabees that seems to clearly teach the reality of purgatory. It reads as follows.

> So they all blessed the ways of the Lord, the righteous judge, who reveals the things that are hidden; and they turned to supplication, praying that the sin that had been committed might be wholly blotted out. The noble Judas exhorted the

people to keep themselves free from sin, for they had seen with their own eyes what had happened as the result of the sin of those who had fallen. He also took up a collection, man by man, to the amount of two thousand drachmas of silver, and sent it to Jerusalem to provide for a sin offering. In doing this he acted very well and honorably, taking account of the resurrection. For if he were not expecting that those who had fallen would rise again, it would have been superfluous and foolish to pray for the dead. But if he was looking to the splendid reward that is laid up for those who fall asleep in godliness, it was a holy and pious thought. Therefore he made atonement for the dead, so that they might be delivered from their sin (2 Maccabees 12:41-45 NRSV).

This passage clearly states that some type of sacrifice can be offered for the dead. The sacrifices and prayers of the living can help those who have died, and are suffering in purgatory.

7. HEBREWS 9:27

The writer to the Hebrews spoke of judgment following death. He put it this way.

And just as it is appointed for mortals to die once, and after that the judgment (Hebrews 9:27 NRSV).

Those who believe in purgatory understand these two events as happening immediately after one another. The person dies and then there is a judgment to determine their destination. The wicked are sent away to hell while the righteous go to either heaven, if they are in a perfected state, or purgatory, if further purification is needed.

From passages such as these, the Roman Catholic Church believes it can find some biblical support for their doctrine of purgatory.

RESPONSE

The verses used to support purgatory do not give credence to this belief. We can make the following observations.

1. ISAIAH 4:4

Isaiah's reference has nothing to do with purgatory. It speaks of God refining people in this life, not the next. Therefore, this is not a reference to purging the believer after this life is over so they can eventually enter into the presence of the Lord.

2. MATTHEW 5:25-26

Paying the last penny has nothing to do with paying for sin in the next life. In Roman law, the plaintiff could bring the accused along with him to the judge. The defendant could however, settle the matter on any terms with the plaintiff as they proceeded to the tribunal. However once they reached the tribunal the issue would be settled according to law. Jesus is encouraging people to settle their differences before it reaches the judge. There is nothing here which remotely suggests a purgatory.

3. MATTHEW 12:32

This passage compares this world and the next and supposedly hints at forgiveness in the next world. However, the phrase "this world and the next" was a Hebrew phrase meaning "never."

Indeed, in the other gospels which give this same account, the phrase is omitted. This is because Mark and Luke are writing for Gentiles. In addition, they each state that the blasphemy of the Holy Spirit will "never be forgiven." Mark says.

> But whoever blasphemes against the Holy Spirit can never have forgiveness, but is guilty of an eternal sin (Mark 3:29 NRSV).

The account in Luke reads.

> Anyone who speaks a word against the Son of Man will
> be forgiven, but the one who blasphemes against the Holy
> Spirit will not be forgiven (Luke 12:10 HCSB).

Nowhere does it state, or imply, that forgiveness can be achieved in the next world. Never means never!

Furthermore, in purgatory sins can supposedly be forgiven. According to Jesus, those who commit the unpardonable sin can *never* receive forgiveness in this world or the next. Consequently, this passage has nothing to do with purgatory. Indeed, the subject is the "unpardonable sin."

4. MATTHEW 18:34

This is a parable about forgiving others. The torture which the man received was in this life, not the next. The debt he owed was to be paid in this world.

In addition, those believers who do not forgive others will suffer in the present life, not in the afterlife. They may lose some of their reward in heaven but they will not be tortured for their lack of forgiveness. Jesus Christ has paid for those sins.

5. 1 CORINTHIANS 3:10-15

"He shall be saved through fire" does not mean he shall be kept alive in the midst of hell-fire. The fire deals with the works of a person, not their character. Some of their works will receive a reward while other of their works will not.

In addition, this testing by fire occurs on judgment day, not in the intermediate state. Judgment day occurs after the person is raised from the dead. Again, we find no purgatory here.

6. 2 MACCABEES 12:41-42, 45

The teaching of a purgatory found in 2 Maccabees has no relevance at all for believers. The reason is that 2 Maccabees is not included in the text of sacred Scripture. Hence anything it teaches is not to be regarded as authoritative. It cannot and should not be used as a source to determine Christian doctrine. This is the first problem with this text.

IT DOES NOT TEACH THE DOCTRINE

Furthermore, this passage does not teach the doctrine of purgatory. For one thing, the word purgatory is nowhere to be found in this passage. Judas and his fellow warriors pray and offer sacrifices for their fallen comrades who had committed the terrible sin of idolatry. No place of purging is mentioned in this passage.

In addition, the passage says that Judas found a pagan idol in the tunic of every dead soldier. He believed that this rebellion against God was what actually caused their death.

Therefore, these soldiers committed what the Roman Catholic Church considers a mortal sin, idolatry. Mortal sins cannot be forgiven! Those who die in mortal sin go straight to hell, not to purgatory. The suffering in purgatory can only forgive venial sins. Consequently, these soldiers were not candidates for purgatory. They died unrepentant having committed a mortal sin.

These points make it clear that this passage cannot be used to substantiate the doctrine of purgatory.

7. HEBREWS 9:27

There is absolutely nothing in verse that mentions, or hints of, a purgatory. Furthermore, it does not specifically say that the judgment comes immediately after death. The Scriptures teach the contrary. Judgment only comes after Jesus Christ returns and resurrects the dead. This is still future.

In addition, the judgment of believers consists of handing out rewards. Thus, judgment day for the Christian is actually "reward day." Hence this verse offers no support whatsoever for any sort of purgatory.

CONCLUSION: THE BIBLE DOES NOT TEACH THE DOCTRINE OF PURGATORY

After looking at the various passages that are used to claim biblical support for purgatory, we find that they do not teach this doctrine. Believers go immediately to be with Jesus Christ upon their death. No suffering is necessary. Purgatory does not exist.

SUMMARY TO QUESTION 17
IS THERE ANY BIBLICAL SUPPORT FOR PURGATORY?

Those who believe in purgatory admit there is no direct support in Scripture for their belief. However, they do insist that there are some biblical passages which are consistent with the idea that believers will suffer for their sins after death before they will be allowed into heaven.

The main support is found in a passage in the apocryphal book of Second Maccabees. This passage speaks of people praying for the dead and offering gifts on their behalf. There are also a number of passages in the New Testament which speak of torturing people until their debts are paid, forgiveness in the next life, and our works tested by fire. While not directly speaking of a purgatory these passages are supposedly consistent with the idea.

However, the passages that purportedly teach this doctrine do no such thing. On the contrary, they contradict any idea that people can pay off certain sins in the next life before entering heaven. The passage in Second Maccabees is in a book which is not part of Holy Scripture. Therefore, it has no authority whatsoever. Furthermore, those who died in that episode had committed the sin of idolatry which is a mortal sin according to the Roman Catholic Church. Mortal sins cannot be forgiven in purgatory!

The New Testament passages refer to suffering and payment of debt in this life, not the next. Thus, they have nothing to do with purgatory.

Jesus' statement about the unpardonable sin not being able to be forgiven in the next life is certainly not speaking about possible forgiveness in the next world or of a future purgatory for Christians. The Scripture is as clear as can be: the unpardonable sin is rejecting Jesus Christ and it can never be forgiven. There is no forgiveness in the next life.

Our works will be tested by fire and some of them will burn up as the Scripture says. But this is referring to our loss of reward, not any suffering for sin. Again, it has nothing to do with personal suffering in some intermediate state between earth and heaven.

Therefore, the biblical evidence which is sometimes used to support the idea of purgatory does not do this. Scripture does not give us the slightest hint that such a state exists. Therefore, we conclude that it does not exist.

QUESTION 18

Why Is Purgatory Such An Attractive Belief For So Many People?

The doctrine of purgatory says that believers in Jesus Christ are not able to go immediately to heaven upon their death because they are not in a state of moral purity or moral perfection. Since the Lord only allows perfection in His presence something must happen to that person before they can enter into heaven. The solution is that they must go to a place of purging before heaven is accessible to them. This place of purging is called purgatory. In purgatory, they are sufficiently purged of their sins so that they will eventually be allowed into heaven.

As we have seen in our previous questions, there is no biblical support for purgatory whatsoever. None. Purgatory does not exist.

If this is the case, then we need to answer the question as to why purgatory holds such an attraction to so many people. Why do people cling to the idea of this place of purging that awaits them after this life? Why do they reject the idea that they can immediately go to heaven upon their death?

THE TWO REASONS FOR THE ATTRACTION

There seems to be two main reasons as to why purgatory, this place of purging, holds such an attraction to humans. First, the belief in purgatory tells us that we can earn our way into heaven. In other words, we can pay for our own sins. Second, purgatory is viewed as a substitute for the doctrine of hell. We can make the following observations.

ATTRACTION 1: WE CAN EARN OUR WAY INTO HEAVEN

Basically, the doctrine of purgatory says that we must pay for our own sins so that we can enter into heaven. While Christ did die for our sins on the cross to make a way for us to go to heaven, we must also pay for them.

This is one of the attractions of purgatory. Paying for our own sins gives us the feeling that we have earned our way into God's presence. We have done something to get there. Purgatory says that I must suffer for my own sins. All of us have guilt for the sins we have committed. We know we are not perfect. Purgatory helps us with our guilty conscience.

Human nature wants to feel like it has earned something. Therefore, if we experience some type of suffering for our sins, this would make us feel better about going to heaven. This is in contrast to accepting God's free gift of salvation by grace apart from any good work which we may do.

THE BIBLICAL RESPONSE: WE CAN DO ABSOLUTELY NOTHING TO EARN OUR SALVATION

Although the idea of salvation by grace, apart from human works, is a difficult concept for prideful humans to accept, it is the clear teaching of Scripture. We can do absolutely nothing to earn our way into heaven. Consequently, as we look at the Scripture we discover there is no support whatsoever for a place called purgatory.

WE DO NOT UNDERSTAND THE DEPTH OF SIN

There is something else. None of us would assume we could earn our way into heaven if we truly understand the nature of sin. Sin is something which God hates with a holy hatred. It is not within our capability to properly pay for it.

ATTRACTION 2: PURGATORY IS SUBSTITUTED FOR HELL

Another reason that purgatory holds a certain attraction to people is that it offsets the idea of hell. Most people do not think that they are bad enough to go to hell. They have the idea that hell is for the truly evil people. Tyrants, mass murderers, those who commit gross sins against children are the ones for whom hell was made. They do not believe that they fit into this category. Consequently, they reject the idea that they will have to go to hell.

On the other hand, these people realize that they are guilty of some sin. Indeed, they are not morally pure to the place where they can enter into heaven. Since they do not qualify for either heaven or hell there must be a third place to go. That place is purgatory. Here, they can get properly prepared for heaven. Purgatory is a type of hell, a kinder, gentler hell.

Thus, purgatory is a subject which can be freely discussed among humans as opposed to the idea of an eternal hell which makes everyone uncomfortable. Our destiny is now manageable.

This also fits their idea of what a God of love would do. Certainly He would not send good people to an eternal hell because of a few imperfections! Instead, upon death, the Lord will send them to this place of purging to get them properly prepared for heaven.

THE BIBLICAL RESPONSE: THERE IS A REAL HELL

While substituting purgatory for hell is truly attractive, it is contrary to what Scripture plainly teaches. There is a heaven, there is a hell. There is no third place. If our sins have not been paid for while we are here upon the earth, then we must pay for them in hell for all eternity. Purgatory does not exist but hell, the lake of fire, certainly does.

THERE IS A NEED FOR PURGING OF OUR SINS BEFORE ENTERING HEAVEN

The idea of purgatory was invented because there was a need for fallen human beings to be cleansed from their sins before entering heaven.

Indeed, God is perfect and there cannot be any imperfection in His presence. The Bible stresses this fact.

> Make every effort to live in peace with everyone and to be holy; without holiness no one will see the Lord (Hebrews 12:14 NIV).

This could not be clearer. Without complete holiness it is impossible to see the Lord.

In the Book of Revelation, we read the words of the Lord as to who will enter into the Holy City, heaven, and who will not. He said.

> Blessed are those who wash their robes, so that they may have the right to the tree of life and may enter the city by the gates. Outside are the dogs, the sorcerers, the sexually immoral, the murderers, the idolaters, and everyone who loves and practices lying (Revelation 22:14,15 HCSB).

Those who wash their robes, the ones free from sin, have the right to eternal life. Again we find the emphasis on purity.

While we agree that purging is indeed necessary to enter into God's presence the Bible makes it clear that this purging has already happened. Jesus Christ took the penalty of the sins of the world upon Himself! The idea of purgation is biblical but the purging is not future. Indeed, it has already happened in the past.

CONCLUSION: WE HAVE ALREADY BEEN CLEANSED

Thus, purging of our sins is certainly necessary before we can enter heaven. With this, we are in agreement with the Roman Catholic Church and the Orthodox Church. However, the good news from Scripture is that we have already been purged! Our sins have been paid for by Jesus Christ. The fact that we need to be purged does not require a place of purging. The purging has already taken place. The writer to the Hebrews emphasized this when he wrote.

Who being the brightness of *His* glory and the express image of His person, and upholding all things by the word of His power, when He had by Himself purged our sins, sat down at the right hand of the Majesty on high (Hebrews 1:3 NKJV).

Jesus has purged our sins by His death on the cross of Calvary.

Paul wrote something similar to Titus where he said.

He gave Himself for us to redeem us from all lawlessness and to cleanse for Himself a special people, eager to do good works (Titus 2:14 HCSB).

Christ gave Himself to redeem us from sin. Indeed, we are cleansed of our sins when we accept His work on our behalf.

Here is the difference between Protestant theology and Roman Catholic and Orthodox theology. Protestantism, following the Scriptures, believes and teaches that we have already been purged of our sins. It is a past act. We have been cleansed.

Therefore, while purgatory may remain an attractive belief for some people, it is contrary to the teachings of God's Word. This is the final standard, the ultimate authority, on all matters of belief and practice. It is important that we hear what it says.

SUMMARY TO QUESTION 18
WHY IS PURGATORY SUCH AN ATTRACTIVE BELIEF FOR SO MANY PEOPLE?

The doctrine of purgatory, the teaching that people must be purged of their sins after they die before they can enter heaven, is indeed popular in many circles. There seems to be two basic reasons for this.

First, if we believe that we have to personally pay some price to enter heaven, then we assume that we have in some way earned the right to go there. This fits well with our pride. We do not like the idea that God has done everything for us. Human beings feel that they must also be able to do something to go to heaven. Suffering for our own sins in purgatory is a way in which we can contribute to our own eternal salvation. That idea appeals to us.

Indeed, all of us feel guilty for things we have done in this life. If we are going to eventually pay for our sins with a little bit of purging, or punishment, we do not really mind. Our guilt feelings in this life will be diminished and we can go on with our lives thinking and believing that entrance to heaven will be partially our own doing. This is certainly an attractive idea.

Attractive or not, the doctrine of purgatory is not biblical. Indeed, Scripture stresses that we can do absolutely nothing to gain entrance to heaven. Our suffering is meaningless as far as taking away sins is concerned. We have zero ability to get to heaven. Jesus Christ has done it all.

In fact, He is the only One who can do anything about it. We cannot earn eternal life by anything that we do or say. We are granted eternal life by belief in Christ.

A second reason as to why purgatory is attractive is that it makes a great substitute for hell. The idea of an eternal hell for lost sinners makes everyone uncomfortable. However, the idea of a place where we are purged of our sins makes us feel much better. Instead of certain people going to hell, they go to a place of purging where God readies them for heaven. This is more in keeping with what many people would assume a God of love would do. Since most people are not bad enough for hell but not good enough for heaven the idea of a third place, purgatory, strikes a responsive chord. This makes purgatory extremely attractive.

Yet again this is not what the Bible teaches. There is a hell where people pay for their own sins and this is the only place in the next world where sins can be paid for. Unless our sins are taken care of in this life by Christ, we will have to pay for them in the next life. However, the payment will not be in a temporary place called purgatory but rather in a permanent place called the lake of fire, hell.

One thing we can agree upon with the Roman Catholic Church and the Orthodox Church is this need for the purging of our sins before we can enter heaven. Indeed, without holiness none of us can see the Lord.

However, the Bible plainly states that this has already happened in the past. We have been purged. Jesus Christ has taken upon Himself the penalty for all of our sins. It is a past completed act. We cannot add to it. All that we can do is accept it by faith. This is what allows us to enter into heaven. It is not by suffering in a mythical place called purgatory; no matter how attractive the concept may be.

What Is Limbo?
(*Limbus Infantum*)

Roman Catholic theology teaches that babies who die without being baptized go to a place on the outskirts of hell called *Limbus Infantum*. These infants can never go to heaven because they have not been baptized in water as Jesus commanded. This command is supposedly found in John's gospel when Jesus spoke to the religious leader Nicodemus. We read.

> Jesus answered, "Very truly, I tell you, no one can enter the kingdom of God without being born of water and Spirit" (John 3:5 NRSV).

This verse supposedly teaches that only the baptized can enter into heaven.

THE BELIEF IN LIMBO

Although these babies do not go to heaven, neither are they tortured. During the Middle Ages the Roman Catholic theologians taught that there was a vast cavity in the center of the earth that was divided into four compartments

1. Hell

2. Purgatory

3. Limbo of infants who died unbaptized

4. Limbo of the fathers

Thus, these children are neither lost nor are they saved.

RESPONSE TO LIMBO

John 3:5 is not referring to water baptism, neither does it have anything to do with infant baptism. Baptism is not an essential requirement of salvation. Paul wrote.

> For Christ did not send me to baptize, but to preach the gospel, not with wisdom of words, lest the cross of Christ should be made of no effect (1 Corinthians 1:17 NKJV).

Paul clearly says that Christ sent him to preach the gospel, he was not sent to baptize. This makes it clear that baptism is not part of the good news of Jesus. Therefore, no such place as *Limbus Infantum* exists.

As we shall see in our book on "Heaven," infants who die go to be with the Lord.

SUMMARY TO QUESTION 19
WHAT IS LIMBO?

Roman Catholic theology teaches that infants who die do not go to heaven or hell but rather to a place called limbo or Limbus Infantum. Supposedly this is located somewhere on the outskirts of hell.

However, the Scripture speaks of no special place for infants who die. The Roman Catholic doctrine of limbo is not found in the Scriptures. Therefore, it is a non-biblical concept. When a person dies they are either with the righteous or unrighteous, they are not in any third place. Indeed, Scripture knows nothing of any "third place" whether it be purgatory or limbo.

In the fourth book of our series on the Afterlife, "Heaven: The Final Destination of Believers," we will discover that infants who die go to heaven.

Should The Living Pray
For The Dead?

We have seen from Scripture that the dead do not cease to exist. Indeed, though the body may die, the spirit lives on in the next world.

This brings up an often-asked question. Does the Bible indicate that the living should ever pray for the dead? Is there any chance that those on earth can help those in the next world?

The Bible is clear on this subject. Indeed, it says that there is no basis whatsoever for the living praying for the dead. The following points can be made.

1. THE CONDITION AFTER DEATH IS DETERMINED IN THIS LIFE

Where we go after we die will be determined in this life alone. Jesus made this plain to the religious leaders of His day when He said the following.

> I told you that you would die in your sins, for you will die in your sins unless you believe that I am he (John 8:24 NRSV).

Our destination in the next life is dependent upon choices made in this life. Unless a person believes in Jesus Christ they will die in their sins.

2. THERE IS NO CHANGE POSSIBLE

Jesus also said that no one could pass from the place of the unrighteous dead to the place of the righteous dead. In the story of the rich man and Lazarus, this was explained to the rich man who was in torment. He was separated from the righteous without any possibility of cross over. Scripture says.

> And besides all this, between us and you a great chasm has been set in place, so that those who want to go from here to you cannot, nor can anyone cross over from there to us (Luke 16:26 NIV).

Once a person enters the afterlife, there is no crossing over from one side to the other. Destinies are forever fixed.

3. AFTER DEATH THERE IS JUDGMENT

The Bible says that after death comes judgment. Condemnation for the wicked and rewards for righteous, not purgatory. The writer to the Hebrews said.

> And just as it is destined that each person dies only once and after that comes judgment (Hebrews 9:27 NLT).

Final judgment is never dependent upon what we do "after" we die. It is only determined on what we do "before" we die.

4. JESUS WEPT FOR HIS DEAD FRIEND

When Jesus came to the tomb of his dead friend Lazarus, the Bible tells us that He wept for Lazarus. Scripture says.

> Jesus wept (John 11:35 KJV).

Notice that the Lord did not pray for him. Prayer wouldn't have made any difference since the fate of Lazarus had already been determined.

5. THE EXAMPLE OF DAVID'S SON

King David prayed fervently for his young son while he was still alive. Once the child died, David stopped praying, for there was nothing else anyone could do. We read David's response in Second Samuel. It says.

David replied, "I fasted and wept while the child was alive, for I said, 'Perhaps the LORD will be gracious to me and let the child live.' But why should I fast when he is dead? Can I bring him back again? I will go to him one day, but he cannot return to me" (2 Samuel 12:22,23 NLT).

The dead cannot return. This is made clear.

6. REWARDS ARE ONLY EARNED IN THIS LIFE

Believers earn their rewards in this life. There is no chance to earn them in the intermediate state. Scripture teaches that we will be judged for our works, and there is no work that we can do to please God after we have died. Works as a basis for our reward are limited to this life.

7. THERE IS NO EXAMPLE OF PRAYING FOR THE DEAD

In addition, we find no example of Scripture of anyone praying for the dead. All the prayers that are offered are for those who are alive. Nowhere are believers commanded to pray for those who have died.

8. IT GIVES PEOPLE A FALSE HOPE

There is something else which must be emphasized. Praying for the dead gives false hope to people. What is worse is that it stops the prayers for the living. This is where our prayers should be directed, not for those who have passed on to the next world. They are beyond our help, beyond our prayers.

On the other hand, the Bible does command us to pray for the living saints. Paul wrote the following command to the Ephesians.

And pray in the Spirit on all occasions with all kinds of prayers and requests. With this in mind, be alert and always keep on praying for all the saints (Ephesians 6:18 NIV).

We are to pray *for* the saints, not to them. Yet all believers are saints. The saints we are to pray for are the living saints; our fellow believers in Jesus Christ.

Thus, there is no purpose in praying for the dead. Those who are with the Lord do not need it and those which are separated from Him cannot benefit by it.

SUMMARY TO QUESTION 20
SHOULD THE LIVING PRAY FOR THE DEAD?

The Bible says that the fate of the dead is determined solely by their actions in this life. There is no change of destiny possible once a person has died. Scripture says after death comes the judgment. In other words, there is not a second chance to believe or to earn favor with God. Therefore, praying for the dead does no good whatsoever.

Indeed, there is not one biblical example of a person or persons praying for the dead. Instead, we find Jesus crying at the tomb of His dead friend Lazarus, but He did not pray for him. Prayer would not have done Lazarus any good.

There is also the example of David's infant son who was gravely ill. David continuously prayed for the child while he was alive. Once he knew that his son was dead, David accepted the fact that nothing else could be done for him. He did not pray for him because he knew his prayers would not have made any difference.

Prayers should be made for the living. We pray for the living saints, the believers in Jesus Christ, not to the dead saints. The deceased cannot be helped by our prayers.

We should, therefore, realize praying for the dead gives people false hope. It gives the impression these people can somehow be helped by our prayers. They cannot. We must realize that Scripture clearly teaches this. Thus, our prayers should concentrate on the living.

Is Onesiphorus An Example Of Praying For The Dead?

There are no examples in Holy Scripture of the living believers praying for the dead. The Bible commands no such practice. However, some claim a biblical basis for praying for the dead in Paul's words about a man named Onesiphorus. The situation is as follows.

DID PAUL PRAY FOR THE DEAD ONESIPHORUS?

When Paul wrote his second letter to Timothy, he mentioned a man named Onesiphorus. Paul asked that the Lord would grant him mercy. He put it this way.

> May the Lord grant mercy to the household of Onesiphorus, because he often refreshed me and was not ashamed of my chain; when he arrived in Rome, he eagerly searched for me and found me—may the Lord grant that he will find mercy from the Lord on that day! And you know very well how much service he rendered in Ephesus (2 Timothy 1:16-18 NRSV).

Some have used this passage to argue for praying for the dead. It is said that Paul prayed for mercy for Onesiphorus, a man who was dead. Therefore, Paul believed his prayer could have some affect on the outcome of the destiny or reward of Onesiphorus.

Consequently, if Paul thought it was right to pray for those who have died, we should be able to do the same. Thus, prayer for the dead is sanctioned in Scripture.

RESPONSE

The following responses can be made to the idea that Onesiphorus is an example of believers praying for the dead.

1. WE DO NOT KNOW THAT HE WAS DEAD

First, we do not know that he was dead. Nothing in this passage makes this certain. The fact that Paul prayed for his entire household does not mean Onesiphorus himself was dead. Therefore, we do not know whether or not this man had died. This is our first point.

2. THIS IS NOT A PRAYER ON HIS BEHALF

Second, even if he were dead, this is not a specific prayer on his behalf. Paul is merely expressing a desire that mercy will be shown to him on the Day of Judgment. Praying for the dead is contrary to everything the Bible teaches.

Furthermore, since nowhere else in Scripture is there the slightest hint that the living are to pray for the dead, we need to interpret this passage in light of this. God does not contradict Himself. We should not expect to find this one passage teaching something which is contrary to the rest of Scripture. A close examination of this passage reveals that it does not.

SUMMARY TO QUESTION 21
IS ONESIPHORUS AN EXAMPLE OF PRAYING FOR THE DEAD?

There have been those that have argued that Paul prayed for a man who was dead named Onesiphorus. In his letter to Timothy, Paul asked that Onesiphorus be granted mercy on the Day of Judgment. This has caused some to assume that Onesiphorus was dead and that Paul was praying on his behalf.

Therefore, it is argued, that believers also may pray for the souls of the departed.

However, this passage about Onesiphorus does not teach that we should pray for the dead for at least two reasons.

First, there is no certainty that he was dead. Nothing clearly states this. Since it is not a foregone conclusion that Onesiphorus was dead at the time when Paul wrote this letter it cannot be maintained that this is a prayer for the dead. We do not know whether or not he was deceased.

In addition, what is recorded is not a specific prayer on his behalf but rather a desire that God would have mercy on this man. There is no special request made for him.

Praying for the dead is not a biblical doctrine. Indeed, we do not find it taught anywhere in Scripture. In fact, when we examine the totality of Scripture we realize that the dead have already had their eternal destiny determined the moment they die. Death brings them to one of two destinations; either in the presence of the Lord or away from His presence. These destinies are forever fixed.

This being the case we should not assume that this passage is the one exception. God does not contradict Himself and He certainly did not contradict Himself in this passage.

Praying for the dead does not help the dead. Their fate has been sealed by their behavior here upon the earth. They are beyond our prayers.

Should The Living Pray To The Dead?

We have found that the Bible does not give us any example of someone praying for the dead. Once a person has died their eternal destiny is forever set. Scripture makes this clear.

This brings up another question about the dead. Though we cannot pray for them, does the Bible allow us to pray "to them?" Should we ever direct our prayers to the believers, the saints, in heaven? Can they help us if we reach out to them.

THE DEAD CANNOT HELP THE LIVING

Again, we discover that the Bible is clear on this matter. We are never instructed to pray directly to someone who has died. Furthermore, there are no examples in Scripture of believers praying to the dead. Indeed, there is no indication whatsoever that they can help us, or that they could even hear our prayers. Praying to the dead is not a biblical practice. Therefore, we should never pray to them because they cannot hear us or help us.

WE SHOULD NOT PRAY TO ANGELS OR OTHER SPIRITUAL BEINGS

In addition, we should never direct any prayers to angels or any other spiritual being that the Lord has created. They have no authority to answer any of our requests.

The Bible says that angels are "ministering spirits" who do the work of the Lord. They are described in this manner.

> Are they not all ministering spirits sent out to serve for the sake of those who are to inherit salvation (Hebrews 1:14 ESV).

Angels do God's bidding, they do not act on their own behalf. Therefore, praying to them cannot accomplish anything.

TO WHOM DO WE PRAY

If we do not pray to the dead, neither to angels or other spiritual beings which the Lord has created, then to whom should we direct our prayers? Simply stated, the Bible says we are to pray to God the Father, through God the Son, by means of God the Holy Spirit.

WE ARE TO PRAY TO GOD THE FATHER

Jesus taught that we are to pray to God the Father. In the Sermon on the Mount, Matthew records Jesus saying the following.

> Pray like this: Our Father in heaven, may your name be honored (Matthew 6:9 NLT).

He also said this to His disciples on the night of His betrayal.

> On that day you will ask nothing of me. Very truly, I tell you, if you ask anything of the Father in my name, he will give it to you (John 16:23 NRSV).

Paul the Apostle also spoke about the necessity of praying to God the Father. He wrote the following to the Ephesians.

> And you will always give thanks for everything to God the Father in the name of our Lord Jesus Christ (Ephesians 5:20 NLT).

Therefore, God the Father is the ultimate One to whom we are praying. This is something which the Scripture makes clear.

JESUS CHRIST IS THE INTERMEDIARY BETWEEN US AND GOD THE FATHER

While we are to address our prayers to God the Father, it is through Jesus Christ that our prayers are heard. In other words, He is our "go-between." The Apostle Paul wrote.

> For there is one God and one intermediary between God and humanity, Christ Jesus, himself human (1 Timothy 2:5 NET).

The writer to the Hebrews said that Jesus is our Great High Priest, our intermediary or "go between." He is the One who brings the prayers to God the Father on our behalf.

> Therefore he had to be made like his brothers and sisters in every respect, so that he could become a merciful and faithful high priest in things relating to God, to make atonement for the sins of the people (Hebrews 2:17 NET).

In the Old Testament, it was the High Priest who represented the people to God. Jesus, our Great High Priest, offers our prayers to the Father.

Scripture is also clear that Jesus understands the problems we face. The writer to the Hebrews emphasized that He can sympathize with us.

> This High Priest of ours understands our weaknesses, for he faced all of the same testings we do, yet he did not sin. So let us come boldly to the throne of our gracious God. There we will receive his mercy, and we will find grace to help us when we need it most (Hebrews 4:15 NLT).

Therefore, He can be sympathetic to our needs because He has had similar experiences.

WE DO NOT PRAY DIRECTLY TO THE HOLY SPIRIT

While the Holy Spirit participates in our prayers, we do not pray directly to Him. Our access to God the Father is through Jesus Christ alone. The Holy Spirit is the one who guides what we should pray; He is not the object of our prayers.

While the Bible does not say that we cannot pray directly to the Holy Spirit, the evidence of Scripture seems to be that we should not pray only to Him.

When believers pray it is to the living God. We address our prayers to God the Father, through God the Son, by means of God the Holy Spirit. Consequently, when we pray, all three members of the Trinity are involved. Jesus Christ is the intermediary between God and humanity.

It is because of His work on the cross as Calvary that believers have access to the living God. He has made it possible that we can pray to Him.

In addition, as our great High Priest, Jesus understands our needs. He is able to sympathize with our sufferings.

While we pray to the Father through the Son, we do not directly pray to the Holy Spirit. He is the one who lives inside each believer and guides our prayers. Consequently we do not direct our prayers at Him.

Conclusion: Prayer Is Directed To God And To Him Alone

In sum, those believers who are in the "in-between" or intermediate state have no ability to help us or even to hear our prayers. Therefore, we should never pray to them or seek them out. The same hold true for angels and all other created beings. We are never to address our prayers to them. Prayers are to be directed to God and to Him alone.

SUMMARY TO QUESTION 22
SHOULD THE LIVING PRAY TO THE DEAD?

While those who have believed in the Lord are in a conscious state of existence in His presence, we on earth should never direct our prayers to them. There is no example of this in Scripture and nothing that encourages such a practice. They cannot help us, only God can.

Neither should we pray to angels. They are merely "ministering spirits" who do the work of the Lord. They have no authority to hear our prayers or answer them. In addition, the other beings the Lord has created, the cherubim, seraphim, and living beings, do not answer our prayers.

Our prayers must be directed to God. We pray to God the Father through God the Son, Jesus Christ. We do this by the leading and guiding of the Holy Spirit. Therefore, our prayers involve each of the three members of the Trinity; the Father, the Son, and the Spirit.

QUESTION 23

What Are The Arguments That The Dead Know What Is Presently Happening On The Earth?

Do people who have died have any idea of what the living are doing? Are they aware of our victories and our defeats? Can they watch our every move? Do they think about us?

Some people believe that the dead do indeed see what is happening here upon the earth. In other words, our dead loved ones know the intimate details as to what is taking place in our daily lives. The biblical arguments for this idea are as follows.

1. THE RICH MAN COULD SEE LAZARUS

The Scripture says that the rich man in Jesus' story could see the dead beggar Lazarus in the unseen world. We read of this in Luke's gospel.

> In Hades, where he was being tormented, he looked up and saw Abraham far away with Lazarus by his side (Luke 16:23 NRSV).

Lazarus was visible to the rich man. The fact that the dead can see others apart from themselves may indicate the dead can view what the living are doing.

2. ABRAHAM KNEW DETAILS OF THE LIFE OF THE RICH MAN AND LAZARUS

Also in this account, we find that Abraham was aware of details of the life of the rich man as well as the beggar Lazarus. We read the following.

But Abraham said, 'Child, remember that you in your lifetime received your good things, and Lazarus in like manner bad things; but now he is comforted here, and you are in anguish' (Luke 16:25 ESV).

Abraham knew that Lazarus had suffered while the rich man lived in comfort without any regard for the needs of others. The fact that he knew these details may give further indication that the dead know what the living are doing.

3. THERE IS A CLOUD OF WITNESSES WATCHING US

The writer to the Hebrews says that the people who are presently living are surrounded by a number of witnesses. He put it this way.

> Therefore since we also have such a large cloud of witnesses surrounding us, let us lay aside every weight and the sin that so easily ensnares us, and run with endurance the race that lies before us, keeping our eyes on Jesus, the source and perfecter of our faith, who for the joy that lay before Him endured a cross and despised the shame, and has sat down at the right hand of God's throne (Hebrews 12:1,2 HCSB).

The witnesses are able to see the believers who are on the earth. Consequently, they know what is happening to us.

4. THE MARTYRS KNEW WHAT HAPPENED ON THE EARTH

The Bible says that the martyrs in heaven knew what was happening on the earth. We read of this in the Book of Revelation.

> When he opened the fifth seal, I saw under the altar the souls of those who had been slain for the word of God and for the witness they had borne. They cried out with a loud voice, "O Sovereign Lord, holy and true, how long before you will judge and avenge our blood on those who dwell on the

earth?" Then they were each given a white robe and told to rest a little longer, until the number of their fellow servants and their brothers should be complete, who were to be killed as they themselves had been (Revelation 6:9-11 ESV).

They wanted to know how long it would take for victory to be granted, for their lives to be avenged. They were told to rest a while longer because the number of the future martyrs was still incomplete. It seems that they could only ask the question because they were observing events here upon the earth, or at the very least, knew what was going one.

In addition, the fact that they were told to rest a while longer further indicates they knew exactly what was happening on the earth.

We also find that those in heaven were conscious that Satan was being defeated. Again, we read of this in the Book of Revelation. It says.

And I heard a loud voice in heaven, saying, "Now the salvation and the power and the kingdom of our God and the authority of his Christ have come, for the accuser of our brothers has been thrown down, who accuses them day and night before our God" (Revelation 12:10 ESV).

They knew Satan had been thrown out of heaven to the earth.

We also find these believers in heaven rejoicing at the fall of Babylon. This is also revealed in the Book of Revelation. It says.

But you, O heaven, rejoice over her fate. And you also rejoice, O holy people of God and apostles and prophets! For at last God has judged her on your behalf (Revelation 18:20 NLT).

These passages are thought to teach that dead can see the living or at least know what they are doing.

SUMMARY TO QUESTION 23
WHAT ARE THE ARGUMENTS THAT THE DEAD KNOW WHAT IS PRESENTLY HAPPENING ON THE EARTH?

There are a number of passages that seem to indicate that the dead presently know what is occurring on the earth. In the story Jesus told of the rich man and Lazarus, we are informed that the rich man could see both Lazarus and Abraham. Furthermore, in that account, Abraham revealed that he knew details of the life of the rich man and Lazarus. This seems to signify that he was aware of what is happening on the earth.

The Book of Hebrews says that a cloud of witnesses is presently surrounding those of us who are living. This may be another indication that the people who are alive on the earth are being observed by the dead.

The Bible, in the Book of Revelation, says the martyrs in heaven know what is going on with the people on the earth. They are aware when Satan is defeated as well as when the city of Babylon falls.

These passages have led many to believe that the dead do know what is presently going on here upon the earth.

What Are The Arguments Against The Idea That The Dead Know What Is Presently Happening On The Earth?

While there are passages that seem to teach that the dead do indeed know what is happening to the living upon the earth, others feel the Scripture does not either teach, or imply, that the dead know what the living are doing. Indeed, they believe that there are better ways to understand these passages.

The main arguments which are given, that the dead do not know what is occurring on the earth, are as follows.

1. THE DEAD DO NOT KNOW ABOUT THIS LIFE

To begin with, there seems to be a number of statements in Scripture about the dead not knowing what the living are presently doing.

In the Book of Job, we find that Job said that the father, who had died, did not know whether his sons were rich or poor. He states it in this manner.

> They never know if their sons grow up in honor or sink to insignificance (Job 14:21 NLT).

Though this could refer to his present earthly knowledge, it may also apply to him in the afterlife.

However, this statement is found in the section of the Book of Job where Job and his friends are trying to determine why Job was suffering so greatly. Later, the Lord would call their discussion "words without knowledge."

Consequently, we must be careful in using any statement from them to determine the truth of what goes on in the next life.

2. THERE IS NO KNOWLEDGE IN THE GRAVE

The Book of Ecclesiastes also says the dead have neither knowledge nor wisdom of what is happening in this life. It says.

> Whatever your hand finds to do, do it with all your might, for in the grave, where you are going, there is neither working nor planning nor knowledge nor wisdom (Ecclesiastes 9:10 NIV).

This passage teaches lack of knowledge on the part of the dead. This, however, may be speaking of things from a human or observational perspective.

From our vantage point here upon the earth, it appears that the dead do not know anything which is going on. Consequently, this passage should not be used to give a definitive answer to the question.

3. ABRAHAM AND JACOB DO NOT KNOW WHAT IS PRESENTLY GOING ON

From a passage in the Book of Isaiah we find that two of the patriarchs, Abraham and Jacob (Israel), do not know what is presently happening upon the earth. In other words, they have no knowledge as to what their descendants are doing. The passage read as follows.

> You are our Father. Even though Abraham doesn't know us and Israel doesn't pay attention to us, O LORD, you are our Father. Your name is our Defender From Everlasting (Isaiah 63:16 God's Word).

This is thought to be another indication that the dead have no knowledge of what is presently happening on the earth.

Again, this statement may only be speaking of something that could possibly happen; not necessarily something that does happen.

In addition, the passage says that Abraham and Israel may not acknowledge or pay attention to the people. This does not necessarily mean that they are unaware of them or what they are doing. Consequently this passage is not conclusive.

4. WE ARE NOT TOLD THAT LAZARUS COULD SEE THE RICH MAN

In the account of the rich man and Lazarus, we are told that the rich man could see Lazarus. However, we are not told that Lazarus could see the rich man. All this says is that unbelievers could see the believers, not the other way around.

In addition, it says nothing about seeing those on earth or knowing what they are doing. The rich man saw Lazarus in the realm of the dead, not the realm of the living.

5. ABRAHAM KNEW DETAILS OF THE RICH MAN AND LAZARUS

Furthermore, in the account of the rich man and Lazarus, Abraham, in heaven, knew of the earthly details of the lives of Lazarus and the rich man. This does not necessarily mean he could see them while they were living or that he was observing their lives.

6. THE CLOUD OF WITNESSES ARE EXAMPLES OF FAITH

The witnesses that are referred to in the Book of Hebrews are the heroes of faith mentioned in Chapter 11. There is no thought whatsoever in this passage of them knowing what is presently occurring on earth.

7. THERE IS NO MORE PAIN IN THE NEXT WORLD

The Bible says the presence of the Lord is a place where there is no suffering or pain for the believer. If, however, the dead in heaven could see what their loved ones are doing on earth, they certainly would be in pain. They would see many of their loved ones on a course to eternal separation from God. This is certainly inconsistent with what the Bible says about the situation of believers in the afterlife; they are in constant joy and happiness.

8. THE EXACT SITUATION WITH THE MARTYRS IN THE BOOK OF REVELATION IS UNCLEAR

The only possible example that we have in Scripture of the dead in heaven knowing what is going on here upon the earth is found in Revelation 6:9-11. In this passage, the souls under the altar cry out for vengeance. Yet there are other explanations of this passage which do not indicate that the dead are watching those on the earth or knowing what people are doing.

Indeed, all we are told is that these martyrs realize that they have not yet have had their deaths avenged. Nothing more. We do not find anything said about their understanding of precise details of what is happening on the earth. They are merely lamenting the fact that the number of martyrs keeps increasing. This of course would lead them to conclude that their deaths have not been avenged. To draw the conclusion that they can see what is happening on the earth is not warranted.

Consequently, while we have a number of arguments which may teach the dead do know what is presently occurring upon the earth there does not really seem to be enough evidence to make a conclusive case. In fact, when we examine the totality of Scripture the idea that the dead know what the living are doing seems unlikely.

ON FINAL POINT: THERE SHOULD BE NO ATTEMPTED CONTACT WITH THE DEAD

Even if one believes that the Bible does teach that the dead know what the living are doing, this should NEVER cause anyone to attempt to reach out and contact them. As we stressed in a previous question, any attempt to do so will result in deception. We again call to mind what the Lord said.

> So why are you trying to find out the future by consulting mediums and psychics? Do not listen to their whisperings and mutterings. Can the living find out the future from the dead? Why not ask your God? "Check their predictions against my testimony," says the LORD. "If their predictions are different from mine, it is because there is no light or truth in them" (Isaiah 8:19,20 NLT).

Therefore, even if one supposes that their dead loved one is watching them here upon the earth this should never be a justification of trying to talk to them. They can be of no help whatsoever to us. We are to talk to the Lord and to Him alone.

SUMMARY TO QUESTION 24
WHAT ARE THE ARGUMENTS AGAINST THE IDEA THAT THE DEAD KNOW WHAT IS PRESENTLY HAPPENING ON THE EARTH?

While there are seemingly some passages in Scripture that may indicate that the dead know what the living are doing there are other passages in Scripture that seem to contradict this idea.

Job said his dead father did not know the status of his living son. Yet this verse does not solve the issue. For one thing, the entire discussion in that section of Job was called "words without knowledge" by the Lord. Furthermore, the statement is made from an earthly perspective. As far as we know on the earth, the dead know nothing. Yet we know from other parts of Scripture that they are conscious in the next world.

The Book of Ecclesiastes says the dead have no knowledge of the living. However, this statement should not be seen as a final answer to this question.

And we can add another thing. There are portions of Ecclesiastes where the author may be saying things contradictory to the teaching of Scripture. He is doing so because of his perspective "under the sun." In other words, without divine revelation we do not know if the dead have knowledge of the living. From our human perspective the dead know nothing at all! Yet Scripture teaches that the dead continue to exist in the afterlife. Thus, this passage does not solve the question.

In a passage in Isaiah, it is claimed that Abraham and Jacob do not presently know what is going on in Israel. Yet this is not the only way to understand the passage. It may be saying that Abraham and Jacob are not concerned with what is happening; not that they do not know

In Jesus' story of the rich man and Lazarus, there is no indication that any of the characters, the rich man, Abraham, or Lazarus could presently see what was currently occurring on the earth. While the rich man could see Lazarus in the realm of the dead, we are not told that he could see his brothers who were still living. Though Abraham knew certain details of the lives of the rich man and Lazarus, this does not mean that he could observe them while he was living.

There is something else which must be considered. It would seem to be inconsistent with the idea of total happiness in the afterlife if the dead know what the living were presently doing. How could they really enjoy the blessings of heaven if they were observing the living in their current state?

The passage in the Book of Revelation where the martyrs are asking the Lord as to when He will avenge their deaths is understood to mean that these dead believers were observing the events upon the earth. But this is not necessarily the case. They merely recognized that more and more martyrs were going to heaven.

Consequently, they realized their deaths had not yet been avenged since the killing was still going on. In fact, nothing specific is said about these deceased believers in heaven knowing any specific details of what is occurring on the earth.

Do the dead believers know what the living are doing? From the totality of Scripture we would have to conclude that this is highly unlikely. Indeed, there is nothing specific in the Bible that indicates this.

Finally, even if someone is convinced that the Bible does teach that the dead know what the living are doing it does not give them any justification of attempting to contact them. Indeed, the Scriptures are clear that the dead cannot truthfully communicate with the living. God forbids this practice of attempting to contact the dead in the strongest of terms.

What Are The Arguments For People Remaining Unconscious After Death? (The Doctrine Of Soul Sleep)

The doctrine of soul sleep teaches that upon death the soul of each person, believer and unbeliever alike, "sleeps" until the general resurrection of the dead and the time of judgment. Though all people will be raised from the dead, the condition of humans between death and the resurrection is one of unconsciousness. The soul is alive but unconscious while waiting the time of the end. Eventually each soul will be awakened to resurrection, and then to judgment.

The arguments given for soul sleep are as follows.

1. DEATH IS CALLED SLEEP

The Bible, in a number of places, speaks of death as sleep. The Bible describes the death of the martyr Stephen in the following manner.

> Then he knelt down and cried out with a loud voice, "Lord, do not charge them with this sin." And when he had said this, he fell asleep" (Acts 7:60 NKJV).

Stephen fell asleep. It is contended that he will remain in that state until the resurrection of the dead.

Jesus referred to death as sleep on two different occasions. In one episode, He told the family of Jairus' daughter that she was not dead but merely sleeping. Jesus said.

> "Go away, for the girl is not dead but sleeping." And they
> laughed at him (Matthew 9:24 ESV).

Again, the dead are asleep.

In another episode, Jesus made it clear that sleep was an analogy for the death of His friend Lazarus. We read the following in the gospel of John.

> These things He [Jesus] said, and after that He said to them,
> "Our friend Lazarus sleeps, but I go that I may wake him up."
> Then His disciples said, "Lord, if he sleeps he will get well."
> However, Jesus spoke of his death, but they thought that He
> was speaking about taking rest in sleep. Then Jesus said to
> them plainly, "Lazarus is dead" (John 11:11-14 NKJV).

Therefore, Jesus used sleep to describe death.

Sleep is a period when people lose consciousness. Hence death, like sleep, is a time of unconsciousness. Believers will see God's face when they awake from sleep, at the resurrection.

The prophet Daniel spoke of the day of the resurrection when the dead would wake from sleep. Scripture says.

> Many of those who sleep in the dust of the earth will awake,
> some to eternal life, and some to shame and eternal con-
> tempt (Daniel 12:2 HCSB).

The sleeping dead will be raised for the final judgment. Thus, it is contended that the Scripture is clear that the dead are asleep, they are not conscious.

2. THE SOUL CANNOT EXIST APART FROM THE BODY

Soul sleep assumes that a physical organism is necessary for consciousness. Human existence depends upon the unity of a body and a soul. A person does not have a soul, they are a soul. No aspect of a human being continues to exist apart from the body. Appeal is made to Scripture to substantiate this. For example, we read in Ecclesiastes.

> Man's fate is like that of the animals; the same fate awaits them both: As one dies, so dies the other. All have the same breath; man has no advantage over the animal. Everything is meaningless. All go to the same place; all come from dust, and to dust all return (Ecclesiastes 3:19,20 NIV).

Humans, like animals, go back to the dust when they die. They have no knowledge of anything. Human existence, therefore, is dependent upon having a body, for without a body humans cannot exist.

Indeed, Adam, the first human, didn't become a living being until the soul or spirit was united with a body. Therefore, it is argued that we need a body to be living.

3. THE DEAD KNOW NOTHING

There are a number of passages in Scripture that say the dead know nothing. In Ecclesiastes, we read a clear statement of the fact that the dead know absolutely nothing. The writer said.

> Whatever your hand finds to do, do it with all your might, for in the realm of the dead, where you are going, there is neither working nor planning nor knowledge nor wisdom (Ecclesiastes 9:10 NIV).

They know nothing because they are asleep.

The Psalmist also spoke of those who are dead going to a place of silence.

> It is not the dead who praise the LORD, those who go down to silence (Psalm 115:17 HCSB).

The dead have no knowledge. This is clear from Scripture.

4. NO RESUSCITATED PERSON RELATED WHAT THEY SAW

There is something else which we should note. If the afterlife consists of conscious existence, then why don't we find those who had been dead relating what they saw and heard? In both testaments we have examples of people who were brought back to life, yet none of them gave any explanation of what it was like in the next world. Since none of these persons gave us an explanation, it is assumed by some that they were unconscious and could not relate anything.

5. THE CRIMINAL ON THE CROSS WAS NOT PROMISED IMMEDIATE PARADISE

Those who teach soul sleep have to re-punctuate the words Jesus said to the dying criminal that was next to Him. In order to refute the idea that the man would be immediately with Jesus in paradise, they punctuate the passage as follows.

> And he said to him, "Truly, I say to you today, you will be with me in Paradise" (Luke 23:43).

Therefore, Jesus, instead of promising this man that he would be immediately with Him in paradise, was merely saying that He is telling this man the truth "today," and not some other time. Paradise was something which will occur in the future, not instantly.

These arguments have convinced many that soul sleep best explains the biblical evidence. However, as we shall see, soul sleep is not a biblical doctrine but rather clearly contradicts what the Bible says about the present state of the dead.

SUMMARY TO QUESTION 25
WHAT ARE THE ARGUMENTS FOR PEOPLE REMAINING UNCONSCIOUS AFTER DEATH? (THE DOCTRINE OF SOUL SLEEP)

The idea that the dead are unconscious, awaiting the resurrection, is called "soul sleep." According to soul sleep those who have died are in a state of non-existence until the Lord wakes them at the resurrection of the dead.

There are a number of arguments that are given in favor of this belief. They can be summarized as follows.

For one thing, death is called sleep in Scripture. Indeed, there are a number of examples in the Bible where people who have died are said to be "sleeping." Since we know that people who are asleep are unconscious then it logically follows that the dead are unconscious.

In addition, it is argued that the soul cannot exist apart from the body. For a person to be alive, they must have a soul and a body. Since the body has died they cannot be alive.

There is something else. According to Scripture the dead know nothing. Indeed, there are a number of passages which clearly say that the dead do not know what is happening upon the earth. It is argued that these verses should solve the issue!

Moreover, in those biblical examples of people who were brought back to life, none of them tell us anything of their experience. Why is this case if they were conscious? Wouldn't we expect to hear their testimony of what the next life was like? However, we hear none.

Finally, contrary to popular belief, Jesus did not promise the criminal that was next to Him on the cross that he would be immediately in paradise. He only emphasized that the man would be in paradise someday, not that particular day

These arguments have led some people to accept the idea of "soul sleep."

Yet none of these arguments have any merit. The biblical evidence is that people who die are immediately conscious in the next world. Soul sleep is not a biblical doctrine. We shall see this as we examine the unbiblical doctrine of soul sleep in our next question.

Is Soul Sleep
A Biblical Doctrine?

Soul sleep is the idea that the dead are in a state of sleep or unconsciousness until they will be awakened at the time of the resurrection
of the dead. While certain passages in Scripture are used to support
this idea, a careful investigation of the Bible will reveal that it does not
teach soul sleep.

Scripture makes it abundantly clear that the souls, or spirits, of both the
saved and the lost are conscious after death. The Bible never states the
souls of the dead are sleeping; it is only their bodies which are asleep.

The biblical evidence is as follows.

1. THE BODIES OF THE DEAD ARE ASLEEP NOT THEIR SPIRITS

To begin with, we should note that when the Bible compares death to
sleep it is speaking of the bodies of the deceased. The bodies of the dead
appear to be sleeping because they have no consciousness or awareness
of what is occurring around them.

Yet believers are no longer in those sleeping bodies. They are said to be
absent from their body immediately upon death but present with the
Lord. Paul wrote the following to the Corinthians.

> We are confident, I say, and would prefer to be away from the
> body and at home with the Lord (2 Corinthians 5:8 NIV).

According to Paul, the spirit is absent from the body but at home or present with the Lord. The spirit and body are separated at death. The spirit is not asleep.

A. STEPHEN'S BODY, NOT HIS SPIRIT, FELL ASLEEP

It is always the body which is said to have fallen asleep; never the spirit of that person. When the martyr Stephen was dying by stoning, he asked the Lord Jesus to receive his spirit. The Bible records it in this manner.

> But he, full of the Holy Spirit, gazed into heaven and saw the glory of God, and Jesus standing at the right hand of God. And he said, "Behold, I see the heavens opened, and the Son of Man standing at the right hand of God." But they cried out with a loud voice and stopped their ears and rushed together at him. Then they cast him out of the city and stoned him. And the witnesses laid down their garments at the feet of a young man named Saul. And as they were stoning Stephen, he called out, "Lord Jesus, receive my spirit." And falling to his knees he cried out with a loud voice, "Lord, do not hold this sin against them." And when he had said this, he fell asleep (Acts 7:55-60 ESV).

From this episode, we discover a number of things. Stephen, as he was about to die saw Jesus waiting to receive him into His presence. Indeed, Jesus is standing at the right hand of God the Father!

Stephen then prayed directly to Jesus and asked Him to receive his spirit. He then asked forgiveness for those who committed this murder and then he fell asleep, or died. In this passage there is a distinction between the body of Stephen which falls asleep and his spirit which goes immediately to be with the Lord.

B. DAVID'S SLEEPING BODY DECAYED

The literal application of sleep is only to the body. David, for example, fell asleep when he died but it was only his body that decayed. The Bible says.

Now this is not a reference to David, for after David had served his generation according to the will of God, he died and was buried, and his body decayed (Acts 13:36 NLT).

The emphasis is that David's body, not his spirit, is what began to decompose. He spirit, being non-physical could not deteriorate or become corrupt.

C. SOME BODIES OF THE SLEEPING DEAD WERE RAISED AT JESUS' RESURRECTION

In another example, a number of the bodies of the sleeping dead saints were raised when Jesus died and then rose from the dead. The Bible records it this way.

The tombs also were opened, and many bodies of the saints who had fallen asleep were raised (Matthew 27:52 NRSV).

Again, it is the bodies which had fallen asleep, not their spirits. Spirits never fall asleep.

2. THE SOUL OR SPIRIT CAN EXIST APART FROM BODY

One of the arguments often made by those who advocate soul sleep is that the spirit cannot exist apart from the body. However, the Bible teaches no such thing. Scripture makes it clear that the soul of the person can exist apart from the body. We find this taught in both testaments.

A. THE OLD TESTAMENT SAYS THOSE IN SHEOL ARE CONSCIOUS

According to the Old Testament, though the body enters the grave, the spirit enters Sheol, the realm of the dead. In Sheol they live a conscious existence. We read about this in the writings of the prophet Isaiah.

Sheol beneath is stirred up to meet you when you come; it rouses the shades to greet you, all who were leaders of the earth; it raises from their thrones all who were kings of the nations. All of them will answer and say to you: 'You too have become as weak as we! You have become like us!' Your pomp is brought down to Sheol, the sound of your harps; maggots are laid as a bed beneath you, and worms are your covers (Isaiah 14:9-11 ESV).

The unbelievers have a conscious existence in the next world.

B. GOD IS THE GOD OF THE LIVING

Jesus made it clear that God was the God of the living when He answered a question about the resurrection that was put to Him by the religious leaders, the Sadducees. He had the following to say about the fate of those who had died.

But now, as to whether the dead will be raised—even Moses proved this when he wrote about the burning bush. Long after Abraham, Isaac, and Jacob had died, he referred to the Lord as 'the God of Abraham, the God of Isaac, and the God of Jacob' (Luke 20:37 NLT).

Jesus was saying that even though these men were long dead physically, they were still alive. By answering the question of the fate of the dead in the way He did, Jesus corrected any idea that the souls of former dead patriarchs were non-existent. Though the final resurrection has not yet taken place, Jesus asserted that they were still alive. He then goes on to say "they live unto him."

So he is the God of the living, not the dead, for they are all alive to him (Luke 20:38 NLT).

This holds true for all who have died. Hence to suggest that somehow these people are still dead is refuted by Jesus.

C. THE BODY WITHOUT THE SPIRIT IS DEAD

James made it clear that the body without the spirit is dead. He wrote.

For as the body apart from the spirit is dead, so also faith apart from works is dead (James 2:26 ESV).

However, the Bible never says the reverse is true; that the spirit cannot live without a body. Indeed, the spirit can and does live apart from a body. This is another indication that the dead are conscious even though their body is in the grave.

3. THE DEAD ARE CONSCIOUS: MOSES AND ELIJAH DID NOT AWAKE FROM SLEEP WHEN THEY SPOKE TO JESUS AT THE TRANSFIGURATION

We also have the account of Moses and Elijah appearing at the transfiguration of Jesus. This is recorded in Matthew 17:1-8 as well as in the Gospel of Mark and the Gospel of Luke. The impression is that Moses and Elijah are coming from a sphere of conscious life to converse with Jesus. There is no indication that they are awakening from some dreamless sleep, or from some sphere which was no better than life here on the earth. This is another sign that the dead are conscious. They are not in some state of sleep.

4. SAMUEL WAS CONSCIOUS IN THE NEXT WORLD

When the Lord refused to speak to King Saul of Israel, Saul resorted to contacting a medium to speak to the dead prophet Samuel. While this practice was forbidden by the Lord, the Lord allowed Samuel to actually appear on this occasion; much to the surprise of the medium. The Bible records it this way.

> The king said to her, "Don't be afraid. What do you see?" The woman said, "I see a spirit coming up out of the ground." "What does he look like?" he asked. "An old man wearing a robe is coming up," she said. Then Saul knew it was Samuel, and he bowed down and prostrated himself with his face to the ground. Samuel said to Saul, "Why have you disturbed me by bringing me up?" "I am in great distress," Saul said. "The Philistines are fighting against me, and God has turned

away from me. He no longer answers me, either by prophets or by dreams. So I have called on you to tell me what to do (1 Samuel 28:13-15 NIV).

Though he had died and his body was in the grave, Samuel was alive in the next world. From the realm of the dead he pronounced judgment upon Saul. This is another example of the dead being conscious.

5. PAUL WAS NOT PERMITTED TO TALK ABOUT HIS EXPERIENCE IN THE NEXT WORLD

While there is no record of any of those who had been dead, and then came back to life, as relating their experiences in the next world, this does not mean they were unconscious. Paul, for example, clearly said that he was not permitted to relate his experience of the time he was in the presence of the Lord. He stated this in his second letter to the Corinthians.

> But I do know that I was caught up into paradise and heard things so astounding that they cannot be told (2 Corinthians 12:4 NLT).

Paul said that he was not permitted to talk about his heavenly experience.

Moreover, the idea that nobody ever spoke of their experience is an argument from silence. We do not know that Lazarus, or some of the other people who were resuscitated, did not ever talk about their experiences. All we know is that their experience was not recorded. This does not mean they had nothing to talk about.

6. THE CRIMINAL NEXT TO JESUS ON THE CROSS WAS IMMEDIATELY IN PARADISE

As to the criminal on the cross, the punctuation argued by those who believe in soul sleep does not make sense. It is true that the oldest existing manuscripts of the New Testament do not contain punctuation marks, and that their punctuation is theoretically possible. However, since they were both dying, there is no other time Jesus could make this statement than "that very day."

Furthermore, His statement is in response to a specific request, "Lord, remember me "when" You come into Your kingdom." The reason Jesus emphasized the man would be with him that day was because of the general belief that the kingdom of God would come at the end of the world. Jesus told him He would enter God's kingdom immediately!

7. THE WORD DEAD IS USED FOR THOSE WHO ARE ALIVE

The word "dead" is used in Scripture of those who exist and are conscious. We can cite the following examples.

A. THOSE WHO LIVE FOR PLEASURE ARE DEAD

The Bible also speaks of people being spiritually dead while they are still alive. Paul wrote the following to Timothy.

> But the widow who lives for pleasure is dead even while she lives (1 Timothy 5:6 NRSV).

Those who live only for pleasure are dead while they are still alive.

B. THE WAYWARD SON WAS LOST

The wayward son was in a state of spiritual death, or separation, from the Lord. It describes him in the following manner.

> For this son of mine was dead and has now returned to life. He was lost, but now he is found. So the party began (Luke 15:14 NLT).

In these instances, the people were alive and conscious when spoken of as being dead. Death was not the end of consciousness or existence.

C. JESUS' TREATMENT OF THE DEAD

Interestingly, Jesus spoke to the dead as if they were still conscious. In the three instances where He brought someone back to life, He spoke directly to the dead person on each occasion. The record is as follows.

LAZARUS

Jesus shouted to Lazarus to come out of the tomb. The Gospel of John records it this way.

> When he had said these things, he cried out with a loud voice, "Lazarus, come out" (John 11:43 ESV).

Lazarus obeyed and came out from the tomb.

THE SON OF THE WIDOW OF NAIN

When Jesus raised the only son of a woman from the city of Nain, He spoke to the dead man. The Bible says.

> Then he walked over to the coffin and touched it, and the bearers stopped. "Young man," he said, "get up" (Luke 7:14 NLT).

The Bible says the young man then came back to life.

THE DAUGHTER OF JAIRUS

The daughter of Jairus was also spoken to. The Bible records the following as to what occurred.

> But he took her by the hand and called out, "Child, get up!" (Luke 8:54 NRSV).

The child then came back to life.

In each of these occasions, Jesus spoke to the dead. In some sense, it seems that they could hear Him. Whatever the case may be, He acted as though they could hear Him.

8. THE WRITER OF ECCLESIASTES DOES NOT SAY THE DEAD ARE UNCONSCIOUS

Ecclesiastes is often quoted as saying the dead lose all consciousness. We read statements such as this.

> Man's fate is like that of the animals; the same fate awaits them both: As one dies, so dies the other. All have the same breath; man has no advantage over the animal. Everything is meaningless. All go to the same place; all come from dust, and to dust all return (Ecclesiastes 3:19,20 NIV).

Yet this passage does not say that humans lose consciousness. In fact the next verse asks the question, "Who knows what happens?" It reads as follows.

> Who knows if the spirit of man rises upward and if the spirit of the animal goes down into the earth? (Ecclesiastes 3:21 NIV).

From a human perspective, nobody does know. Yet the God of Scripture certainly knows and He tells us; the dead do not lose consciousness.

Another favorite passage for soul sleep is found later in Ecclesiastes. It reads.

> For the living know that they will die, but the dead know nothing; they have no further reward, and even the memory of them is forgotten (Ecclesiastes 12:5 NIV).

The writer says the dead do not know anything. Again, this is true from a human perspective. The dead bodies do not know what is occurring around them. This, however, is not to say that their spirit, the real part of them, is unconscious and unaware of their present surroundings.

In fact, the writer makes it clear two verses later that the body goes to the ground or the dust while the spirit goes back to God. He wrote.

The dust returns to the ground it came from, and the spirit returns to God who gave it (Ecclesiastes 12:7 NIV).

The writer understands that it is the body which returns to the elements from which it was created, dust. This, however, says nothing about the spirit. Indeed, our spirits were not made out of dust! The spirit returns to God and the spirit is conscious.

Therefore, statements in Ecclesiastes should not be used to argue for "soul sleep" as a biblical teaching. It is not.

9. GOD, ANGELS, CHERUBIM, SERAPHIM, THE LIVING CREATURES ARE SPIRIT BEINGS: THEY EXIST WITHOUT PHYSICAL FORM

God is Spirit, and so are the other created beings the Scripture speaks of; angels, cherubim, seraphim and the living creatures. Neither has any physical form. Jesus said the following about God.

God is spirit, and those who worship him must worship in spirit and truth (John 4:24 ESV).

While God has no physical or corporeal form He certainly consciously exists!

Angels are also spirits. The writer to the Hebrews testified.

But angels are only servants. They are spirits sent from God to care for those who will receive salvation (Hebrews 1:14 NLT).

Angels, though spirit-beings also have a consciousness existence. The same holds true of the other spirit-beings in which the Lord has created; cherubim, seraphim and the living creatures. Therefore, beings without a body can exist in a conscious state.

10. HOW COULD PAUL BE FAR BETTER OFF WHEN DEAD?

If Paul was asleep at death, how could he say that to die, and to be with the Lord, was far better than being in this body? He wrote this to the Philippians.

I find it hard to choose between the two. I would like to leave this life and be with Christ. That's by far the better choice (Philippians 1:23 God's Word).

Conscious fellowship with the Lord in this life would be better than being unconscious in the next. Yet that was not what Paul was expecting. Indeed, he was expecting to be conscious after death.

11. THE SPIRITS OF THE RIGHTEOUS ARE WITH THE LORD

The Bible says the spirits of the righteous are already with the Lord. We read the following in the Book of Hebrews.

> You have come to the assembly of God's firstborn children, whose names are written in heaven. You have come to God himself, who is the judge of all people. And you have come to the spirits of the redeemed in heaven who have now been made perfect (Hebrews 12:23 NLT).

These perfected spirits are certainly not asleep or unconscious!

We read of this in the Book of Revelation. It says.

> And I heard a voice from heaven saying, "Write this down: Blessed are those who die in the Lord from now on. Yes, says the Spirit, they are blessed indeed, for they will rest from their hard work; for their good deeds follow them (Revelation 14:13 NLT).

Those who have died are promised to be in God's presence. They are not asleep somewhere waiting to be awakened at some future time.

Are we to assume that those who have entered into God's presence are not taking part in all the blessings of the next realm? Why bring them into God's presence and not allow them any of the benefits?

12. THE DEAD ARE ALREADY AWAKE

A number of passages speak of believers being already awake in God's presence. We can consider the following.

A. THERE ARE SOUL'S CRYING OUT IN THE PRESENCE OF THE LORD

The souls of dead believers were crying in God's presence. We read the following in the Book of Revelation.

> They cried out with a loud voice, "Sovereign Lord, holy and true, how long will it be before you judge and avenge our blood on the inhabitants of the earth?" (Revelation 6:10 NRSV).

Were these souls crying in their sleep?

B. THE UNBELIEVERS ARE ALSO CONSCIOUS

From the account that Jesus gave of the rich man and Lazarus (Luke 16:19-31) we discover that unbelievers are also conscious when they are dead. The unbeliever in this account knew who he was, who Lazarus was, who Abraham was, and the fact that he had five brothers. He was completely conscious and had a memory of his past life.

Furthermore, we are told that God is continuing to punish the wicked dead. Peter wrote that the unrighteous are kept under punishment until judgment day. He said.

> So you see, the Lord knows how to rescue godly people from their trials, even while keeping the wicked under punishment until the day of final judgment (2 Peter 2:9 NLT).

The unrighteous are kept under punishment while waiting their final judgment. They are not asleep.

When Jesus spoke of the resurrection of the dead, He spoke of the dead, both righteous and unrighteous, hearing His voice. He said.

Do not be amazed at this, for a time is coming when all who are in their graves will hear his voice and come out—those who have done good will rise to live, and those who have done evil will rise to be condemned (John 5:28-29 NIV).

How could those who are dead "hear" His voice? They will hear Him because they consciously exist.

Therefore, when all the evidence is considered, we find that the doctrine of "soul sleep" is not a biblical doctrine. The dead, both righteous and unrighteous, are conscious in the next world. It is the body which dies, never the spirit or the soul.

SUMMARY TO QUESTION 26
IS SOUL SLEEP A BIBLICAL DOCTRINE?

The doctrine of "soul sleep" says the souls, or the spirits, of the dead are presently unconscious. Since death is compared to sleep in the Bible, it is contended that the dead are now sleeping, waiting to be awakened at the time of the resurrection of the dead.

The Bible however, does not support this contention. While the body is said to be asleep at death, the spirit or soul continues to live in conscious awareness. In fact, the Bible never says that the spiritual part of us goes to sleep. Instead, the Scripture clearly teaches that the believing dead are conscious in the presence of the Lord while the unbelieving dead are conscious apart from Him. The spirit or soul can and does exist apart from the body.

For example, Moses and Elijah appeared with Jesus at His Transfiguration though Moses had been dead for some 1,400 years and Elijah had left the earth some 800 years previously. There is no indication that they awoke from some special state of sleep when they appeared with Jesus. Neither should we assume that they went back to sleep after the Transfiguration.

The dead prophet Samuel spoke to Saul when Saul attempted to contact him through a medium. Samuel was conscious in the next world. There is no indication that he was asleep.

We find that the criminal which was crucified next to Jesus was promised that he would be in paradise that very day. Jesus said "today" they would be together in paradise. No idea of sleeping or waiting was present in Jesus' promise to this dying criminal.

Though no biblical character who came back from the dead relates his or her experience in the next world this certainly does not mean they were unconscious. Paul, for example, who went to the realm of the dead and came back, said that he was not allowed to explain exactly what it was like. But he did say that he saw and heard wonderful things. This surely indicates that he was not unconscious or asleep.

The word "dead" is sometimes used in Scripture for those who are alive. This is the case because the main idea behind death is separation, not extinction or annihilation. Therefore, someone can be dead or separated from the Lord while they are still alive. Death is not extinction or cessation of existence.

While there are many passages in Ecclesiastes which are cited to prove "soul sleep," none of these actually teach the doctrine. In context, they do not teach that the soul becomes unconscious at death. Usually they speak of the dead from the vantage point of one here upon the earth. From our perspective, we do not know what happens to the dead. It is only through divine revelation that we discover the dead are conscious in the afterlife.

Furthermore, the idea that we need a body to be alive in the next world is refuted by the biblical description of both God and the various spirit-beings which He created; angels, cherubim, seraphim and the living creatures. God is a spirit being as are these spirit-beings. They all exist in the unseen world as complete, fully-functional beings without having any physical form.

The Apostle Paul also told the Philippians that when he died he would be with Christ. There is no indication whatsoever in his writings that he thought he would be unconscious at any time. In fact, Scripture emphasizes that the spirits of the righteous are presently with the Lord. Indeed, a number of passages teach that the dead are already awake in His presence.

When all these facts are considered it becomes clear that soul sleep is not a biblical doctrine and consequently it should be rejected as an option for Bible believers.

QUESTION 27

In What Sense Is Death Like Sleep?

Although the doctrine of soul sleep is not taught in Scripture, the Bible does compare death with sleep. The comparison between the biblical idea of death and sleep is appropriate because they have a number of things in common. They include the following.

1. THEY ARE BOTH INEVITABLE

Sleep and death are inevitable. At the end of each day the human body needs sleep. Likewise at the end of our earthly time, the body sleeps in death. Though we may try to fight them, both sleep and death will eventually win.

2. IT IS REST FROM LABOR

Sleep, as well as death, is a state where people have ceased from their labor. It is a time when the body is at rest. No work on this earth is done during sleep or death.

3. IT IS NOT CESSATION OF BEING

Though a person is not working while they are asleep, there is no cessation of being. The mind continues to work while the body sleeps. The person who is asleep has not ceased to exist. Neither is the person who has died.

4. THE AWAKENING COMES AFTERWARD

Those who are asleep, and those who are dead, do not sleep forever. They are waiting for the time when they will again awake. The dead have rested from their earthly labors and are now waiting for the day of their resurrection. This is the time their spirits and bodies will reunite.

5. WE AWAKE TO SOMETHING NEW

As the person who awakes from sleep faces the challenge of a new day, those who awake from the sleep of death begin a new existence. With a resurrected body they will begin life anew. In this case, it is eternal life.

These are some of the ways which we can compare the sleep or rest, which the body needs, with death. Indeed, there are a number of striking comparisons.

SUMMARY TO QUESTION 27
IN WHAT SENSE IS DEATH LIKE SLEEP?

Though death and sleep are not identical, they do have many things in common. Since the Scriptures use sleep as an analogy of death, there are lessons that we can learn from comparing the two. They are as follows.

For one thing, both sleep and death are inevitable; they come at the end of a period of work. At the end of the day we sleep while at the end of our lives we die.

In addition, sleep and death are where people rest from their labors. Though death and sleep are a time of rest, they are not a cessation of being. Those sleeping are still alive and the dead are alive in the afterlife.

Those who are dead, as well as those who are asleep, look forward to a time when they will awake.

Finally, both the dead, and those who are asleep, awake to face something new. In the case of the believing dead, it will be a new, glorified body in which to spend eternity.

Again, we emphasize that Scripture teaches that it is only the body which sleeps. The spirit or soul of a human being never ceases to exist or loses consciousness after this life is over. While death may be compared to sleep in certain ways, death is not sleep.

What Is Reincarnation?

One of the popular beliefs that humans have held in the past, and continue to hold in the present, is that of "reincarnation." It is also called *metensomatosis* which literally means "the changing of bodies." This belief teaches that people can, and do, come back from the dead as another person. This reincarnation occurs in a number of successive lifetimes.

In other words, all of us come back as different people, in different places, and at different times in history. The human soul never really dies or perishes but rather keeps coming back in different forms.

THE MAIN BELIEFS OF REINCARNATION

It is important that we understand exactly what reincarnation is saying about the nature of the world, God, and human beings. We can summarize the main teachings of the doctrine of reincarnation as follows.

1. ALL IS ONE (MONISM)

For those who hold to the belief in reincarnation their view of the world is known as "monism." This can be simply defined as follows. All of reality is seen as a unified whole. Everything which exists belongs to a one single system. This includes any idea of God. God is basically identified with everything which exists. In other words, God is everything and everything is God. There is no idea of God as a personal being in the belief system of reincarnation.

2. PEOPLE COME BACK AS OTHER HUMAN BEINGS: IT IS NOT THE SAME AS TRANSMIGRATION OF SOULS

Reincarnation is different from the doctrine of "transmigration of souls." Transmigration of souls holds that the dead do come back to life but they do not necessarily come back as other humans. Depending upon our behavior, we can come back to this world in another life as animals or plants as well as humans. Thus, a person could conceivably come back to this world as an aardvark or a cactus!

Reincarnation, as it is popularly understood, says that we come back as other humans. It teaches the survival of the self occurs in successive afterlives as other human beings.

3. OUR PAST BEHAVIOR AFFECTS WHO WE ARE TODAY (THE LAW OF KARMA)

Reincarnation is closely linked with what is known as the law of karma. Simply stated, the law of karma says that our past lives have implications on our present life. It is the law of cause and effect. In some sense, the conduct of one's past lives will influence the kind of lives the person will supposedly have in the future. If we have been a good person performing good deeds, then we will come back in the next life in a better situation than if we lived a life characterized by bad deeds. In other words, we can help ourselves by our good behavior.

In the Western view of reincarnation, this law of sowing and reaping continues without end until a person reaches their goal of ultimate perfection or eternal bliss. Often this eternal bless or perfection is called "nirvana." The person becomes one with the universe and the cycle of reincarnation is ended.

However, some views of the law of karma, especially in the East, do not allow the possibility of reaching some state of perfection or bliss.

Instead, humans are doomed to forever experience suffering by a series of endless births and rebirths. Life is suffering and humans are meant to suffer over and over again in various lives. Since perfection is not possible, there is no way to escape reincarnation. There are a number of people who hold this pessimistic view of life.

4. THE SO-CALLED EXPERIENCE OF PAST LIVES IS APPEALED TO AS EVIDENCE OF REINCARNATION

There is something else. People often testify of personal memories which they have had of past lives. They remember being somewhere or doing something at another place, in another time, and as another person. This, they allege, gives further credence to the idea that each of us live a succession of lives.

This is a general summary of the main points of the doctrine of reincarnation.

PRACTICAL IMPLICATIONS ASSOCIATED WITH REINCARNATION

The belief in reincarnation is not something that is merely theoretical. Indeed, it has a number of practical implications. They can be listed as follows.

1. WITH REINCARNATION THERE IS NO GOD

The belief in a personal God is foreign to the teaching of reincarnation. Since all reality is one, there is no idea of God as a personal being. In short, the traditional understanding of God, as a being who exists separately from the universe, is not true. God does not exist.

2. HUMANS HAVE NO INDIVIDUAL EXISTENCE

Another result of reincarnation is the lack of any type of individual existence for human beings. Instead, we are part of one giant unity, the universe. While we may believe we have an individual personality this is not the case. We have existed previously as other people and we will again exist in the future as different individuals. Therefore, the idea of an individual "self" is not found in a world which believes in reincarnation.

3. DEATH IS NOT TO BE FEARED

Since all of us come back to earth as different people at different times, death is not an enemy. It is not to be feared because it is the gateway to another life here upon the earth. Reincarnation, therefore, removes all fear of death.

4. THERE IS NO PERSONAL JUDGMENT AT THE END OF THIS LIFE

Judgment by a personal God is not included in the system of reincarnation. Indeed, since no personal God exists, and there is the belief that we save ourselves by our good behavior in successive lifetimes, the idea of a general judgment of the human race is excluded.

This being the case, the doctrine of hell, or the place of eternal separation from God, is also excluded from the belief system of reincarnation. Any judgment which occurs takes place as we move from one lifetime to another.

This briefly sums up the teaching of reincarnation. As we shall plainly see, it contradicts Scripture in all of its main beliefs.

SUMMARY TO QUESTION 28
WHAT IS REINCARNATION?

Reincarnation is the belief that human beings live a number of lives as different people until they reach a state of perfection or eternal bliss. Therefore, this life which we are now living is only one of a number of possible lives according to those who believe in reincarnation. There were many lives in the past and there will be many more to live in the future.

There are a number of practical implications associated with the belief in the doctrine of reincarnation.

First and foremost is that God does not exist. If the entire universe is one entity, then, by definition, there can be no such thing as a personal God who exists. We are all part of the universe.

We also have to redefine who we are as human beings. Individual identity is a myth if reincarnation is true. While we may have an identity now, we did not have this same identity in previous lives and we will not have it in future lives. Therefore, none of us are limited to the present identity which we now have. We were other people, we shall be other people.

Reincarnation removes a number of fears from humans. For one thing, death no longer holds any fear to a person if reincarnation is true. In fact, death is a part of our reaching a state of perfection. If we have had sufficient good works in this life, then our next life will be better than this one. Therefore, death is something we can look forward to if we have lived a decent life.

Finally, the doctrine reincarnation removes any fear of punishment by a personal God. Since no personal God exists and we pay for our own misdeeds in successive lives, we have no fear of any type of final judgment or accounting for our behavior. Hell does not exist because there is no God to punish us. Our punishment takes place after this life is over and before the next one begins.

What Biblical Arguments Are Given For The Idea That Humans Live A Succession Of Different Lives? (Reincarnation)

Some reincarnationists actually point to Scripture to support their belief. Those advocating the doctrine of reincarnation say that there are several texts in the Bible which sustain their view, or at least are consistent with their view. We can make the following observations.

SOME TEXTS SUPPORTING REINCARNATION WERE SUPPOSEDLY REMOVED FROM SCRIPTURE

While there are people who believe in reincarnation which cite the Bible to prove their point, some reincarnationists make the claim that other texts which support this doctrine were actually removed from Scripture. Yet, even without these removed texts, they see evidence of belief in reincarnation by Jesus Christ and the biblical authors. The biblical evidence for reincarnation is allegedly as follows.

1. THERE IS KNOWLEDGE BEFORE BIRTH (JEREMIAH 1:4-5)

Certain passages speak of knowledge before birth. In the Book of Jeremiah, the Lord said the following to the prophet.

> The word of the LORD came to me, saying, "Before I formed you in the womb I knew you, before you were born I set you apart; I appointed you as a prophet to the nations" (Jeremiah 1:4,5 NIV).

God knew Jeremiah before He was born. This speaks of knowledge before birth. This is a major belief in the system of reincarnation.

2. THERE IS A PREEXISTENT STATE FOR HUMANS (GALATIANS 1:15-16)

There are certain passages that seem to speak of a state of preexistence of the individual. Paul wrote the following to the Galatians.

> But God, who appointed me before I was born and who called me by his kindness, was pleased to show me his Son. He did this so that I would tell people who are not Jewish that his Son is the Good News (Galatians 1:15,16 God's Word).

The fact that Paul spoke of being "appointed before he was born" is supposedly a sign that his spirit, or soul, existed before he was conceived.

The psalmist also spoke of a preexistent state of humans. He spoke of being known while he was being formed in the womb.

> You made all the delicate, inner parts of my body and knit me together in my mother's womb. Thank you for making me so wonderfully complex! Your workmanship is marvelous-and how well I know it. You watched me as I was being formed in utter seclusion, as I was woven together in the dark of the womb. You saw me before I was born. Every day of my life was recorded in your book. Every moment was laid out before a single day had passed (Psalm 139:13-16 NLT).

Therefore, it is concluded by reincarnationists that there is life before birth.

3. JESUS' TESTIMONY OF JOHN THE BAPTIST AND ELIJAH (MATTHEW 17:10-13)

One of the favorite texts of reincarnationists concerns the identity of John the Baptist. It is contended that John the Baptist was actually the reincarnation of the Old Testament prophet Elijah. The Gospel of Matthew records the following account.

So the disciples questioned Him, "Why then do the scribes say that Elijah must come first?" "Elijah is coming and will restore everything," He replied. "But I tell you: Elijah has already come, and they didn't recognize him. On the contrary, they did whatever they pleased to him. In the same way the Son of Man is going to suffer at their hands." Then the disciples understood that He spoke to them about John the Baptist" (Matthew 17:10-13 HCSB).

From this passage, it is alleged that Jesus claimed that John as actually Elijah.

4. PEOPLE NEED TO BE BORN AGAIN THE CYCLE OF REBIRTH (JOHN 3:3)

Jesus told one of the leading religious leaders of His day, Nicodemus, that he needed to be born again. We read of this in John's gospel.

Jesus answered him, "Truly, truly, I say to you, unless one is born again he cannot see the kingdom of God" (John 3:3 ESV).

Born again supposedly refers to the cycle of births in the process of reincarnation. Jesus said to reach eternal bliss one must continually experience these rebirths. Therefore, it is argued that Jesus supported the idea of reincarnation.

5. JESUS' DISCIPLES BELIEVED IN REINCARNATION: THE QUESTION ABOUT THE MAN BORN BLIND (JOHN 9:1-3)

There is also an account which Scripture gives us of Jesus responding to a question about a man who was born blind. The Bible says the following.

As he walked along, he saw a man blind from birth. His disciples asked him, "Rabbi, who sinned, this man or his parents, that he was born blind?" Jesus answered, "Neither

this man nor his parents sinned; he was born blind so that
God's works might be revealed in him" (John 9:1-3 NRSV).

The way the disciples asked the question is instructive. They assumed
it was possible for this man to have sinned in some previous life so as
to have been born blind in this life. Consequently, they believed that
people can come back to this life after living previous lives.

6. MELCHIZEDEK IS AN EXAMPLE OF REINCARNATION (HEBREWS 7:3)

There is a shadowy figure in the Old Testament with the name of
Melchizedek. He appears and disappears quickly on the pages of
Scripture. This ancient king is used as an example of reincarnation. We
read the following about him in the Book of Hebrews.

> He is without father or mother or genealogy, having neither
> beginning of days nor end of life, but resembling the Son of
> God he continues a priest forever (Hebrews 7:3 ESV).

Notice that the Bible says that Melchizedek was without beginning, or
end. This is supposedly an example of reincarnation. It must mean that
he has had lived a number of successive lives as different people and
would continue to live more lives.

7. JOB WILL RETURN TO HIS MOTHER'S WOMB (JOB 1:20-21)

The patriarch Job said that he would return to his mother's womb. This
is often used as a proof text for reincarnation. We read the following in
the Book of Job.

> Then Job arose and tore his robe and shaved his head and fell
> on the ground and worshiped. And he said, "Naked I came
> from my mother's womb, and naked shall I return. The Lord
> gave, and the Lord has taken away; blessed be the name of
> the Lord"(Job 1:20-21 ESV).

Job says he will return to his mother's womb naked. This is alleged to support the idea of returning to the womb for the endless cycle of rebirths.

8. THE WHEEL OF BEGINNINGS SPEAKS OF REINCARNATION (JAMES 3:6)

In the Book of James, we find that James made a statement about the wheel of beginnings. This infers reincarnation. He said.

> And the tongue is a flame of fire. It is a whole world of wickedness, corrupting your entire body. It can set your whole life on fire, for it is set on fire by hell itself (James 3:6 NLT).

An alternative translation of the phrase "your whole life" is the "wheel of beginnings." This is used by reincarnationists for biblical support that individuals get on the wheel of reincarnation. This wheel, they believe, refers to a succession of lives.

9. A PERSON REAPS WHAT THEY SOW: THE LAW OF KARMA (GALATIANS 6:7)

Paul wrote to the Galatians about the laws of sowing and reaping. This is the law of cause and effect. He said.

> You will always reap what you sow! (Galatians 6:7 NLT).

This is cited as the law of karma in action. There is a basic law of cause and effect in the universe and this is recognized by the biblical writers. A person will reap what they sow in this life which will determine who they are in the next life.

10. THOSE WHO TAKE UP THE SWORD WILL DIE BY THE SWORD (MATTHEW 26:52)

Jesus said that those who take up the sword will die by the sword. This is a practical example of the law of karma.

> "Put your sword back in its place," Jesus said to him, "for all who draw the sword will die by the sword" (Matthew 26:52 NIV).

Jesus' statement about dying by the sword is karma in action. A person will reap what they sow, they will pay for their own sins.

11. CERTAIN PEOPLE MUST GO INTO CAPTIVITY AND BE KILLED WITH THE SWORD (REVELATION 13:10)

There is also a statement found in the Book of Revelation about people going into captivity and being killed with the sword.

> If anyone is to go into captivity, into captivity he will go. If anyone is to be killed with the sword, with the sword he will be killed (Revelation 13:10 NIV).

This is supposedly another illustration of the law of karma. There is cause and effect built into the universe. It says "if anyone is to be killed with the sword, he will be killed." Therefore, we have an illustration of the law of karma in the Book of Revelation.

THESE PASSAGES DO NOT TEACH THE DOCTRINE OF REINCARNATION

These are the some of the popular passages which are cited by reincarnationists to illustrate that the biblical writers believed and taught the doctrine of reincarnation.

However, the passages cited do not begin to teach what they claim. Neither is there any evidence that certain passages were removed by church authorities. We will examine their claims in detail in the next couple of questions.

SUMMARY TO QUESTION 29
WHAT BIBLICAL ARGUMENTS ARE GIVEN FOR THE IDEA THAT HUMANS LIVE A SUCCESSION OF DIFFERENT LIVES? (REINCARNATION)

The doctrine of reincarnation states that human beings come back to earth in successive lives as different people. Each time the individual comes back as a different person in a different historical era. It is argued that each of us may have been someone else in a past life. Consequently, we will be someone else in our next life. There is an endless cycle of births, deaths, and re-births. This cycle will go on and on and on.

Reincarnationists often use the Bible to support their idea. Indeed, they cite a number of references in Scripture which supposedly advocate reincarnation. Furthermore, they argue that many of the texts which supported reincarnation were actually removed from Scripture. However, they claim a number of them still remain.

For example, they say the Bible teaches that there is actual knowledge before birth. Scripture says that God knew the prophet Jeremiah before he was even born. This indicates that Jeremiah must have been in some pre-existent state.

The fact that Jesus Christ said John the Baptist was Elijah is supposedly another evidence of reincarnation. John was Elijah in another lifetime. This is classic reincarnation.

They also contend the Jesus' disciples believed in some type of reincarnation with their question about a man who had been born blind. They asked Jesus if it was this man's sin that caused him to be born blind. The question assumes he lived in a previous lifetime where he sinned. His sin caused blindness in the life he lived at the time of Christ.

Jesus Himself told the religious leader Nicodemus that he must be born again. It is said that born again means that a person has to come back to this earth in another body as a different person, or reincarnation.

The Old Testament character Melchizedek is often used an example of reincarnation. Scripture says he did not have any father or mother. In other words, he keeps coming back to the earth as a different person. His appearance on the pages of Scripture is supposedly an example of reincarnation.

The New Testament writer James spoke of the wheel of life. This is often seen as a reference to reincarnation. Each of us is on the wheel as we experience multiple births and rebirths. Some forms of reincarnation teach that it is possible to get off the wheel, or cycle of life, while other forms of this doctrine believes and teaches that these cycles are endless.

These passages supposedly give biblical evidence for the doctrine of reincarnation. However, they do no such thing. Scripture gives no indication whatsoever that people live a number of successive lives as different individuals or that they will come back in future lives as other people. Indeed, as we shall clearly seen in our next few questions, there is no evidence whatsoever from Scripture of any doctrine of reincarnation or that certain passages were removed from the Bible that taught this doctrine.

Do Humans Come Back In Other Lives As Different People? (Reincarnation) What Does The Bible Say About This Subject?

Reincarnation is the belief that we humans live a number of different lives as different people. Each of us has existed at another time, in another place, as another person. The Bible, as well as personal experience, is appealed to when making this claim. Does the idea of reincarnation square with Scripture? How should we respond to the claims made by those who believe in reincarnation? There are a number of points which we need to make.

1. THE BIBLICAL WORLDVIEW IS FOREIGN TO THE IDEA OF REINCARNATION

To begin with, while we will look at a number of biblical proof texts used by reincarnationists and find them to be contradictory to Scripture, the real problem with reincarnation is not the citing of isolated texts in Scripture to support their belief. The real problem with reincarnation is that it contains a view of reality which is totally opposed to the teaching of Scripture. Everything which Scripture teaches about God, human beings, the world we live in, the doctrine of sin and salvation is contradictory to the tenets of reincarnation. In short, the world which the Bible portrays is totally different than the world reincarnationists believe in. It is crucial that we understand this.

We can now make the following specific observations about the doctrine of reincarnation and the Holy Scriptures.

2. THE WORLD IS NOT ONE SINGLE REALITY: A PERSONAL GOD DOES EXIST

Contrary to those who believe in reincarnation, the world does not consist of one reality. The Bible says that the world was created by a personal God who exists apart from the universe. In other words, God existed before the world was made.

The very first verse of the Bible tells us this!

> In the beginning God created the heaven and the earth (Genesis 1:1 KJV).

God created the world. It did not exist before He made it. The God of the Bible is separate from the world. He does not need the world and He is not part of the world.

3. THE GOD OF SCRIPTURE CONTROLS DESTINIES: HUMANS OR FATE DO NOT CONTROL THEM

Furthermore, the God of the Bible is personally involved in this world. He does not sit idly by, merely watching what occurs. Instead, He is intimately involved in the workings of the universe.

In addition, He is in control of all things. Reincarnation does not allow for God to exist; let alone be the One who is in control. According to reincarnation, we are in control of our own fate. This idea is foreign to Scripture.

4. HUMAN BEINGS HAVE INDIVIDUAL IDENTITIES

The Bible also says humans have an individual identity. Indeed, Scripture says that the first humans, Adam and Eve, were the high-point of God's creation being created in God's image and likeness. Reincarnation must reject any idea of a Creator God who made human beings as special.

5. GOD PUNISHES EVIL AFTER ONE LIFETIME

The Bible also teaches that God punishes evil while reincarnation teaches that we will work out our own salvation. Consequently, there will be no judgment day for the human race. Again, this contradicts the teaching of Scripture. There is not another chance to do anything after this life is over. Our destinies are forever set.

CONCLUSION: REINCARNATION AND SCRIPTURE HAVE TWO DIFFERENT VIEWS OF THE WORLD

The evidence is clear; Scripture and reincarnation are two different ways of looking at the world around us. They cannot be reconciled. One of them must be wrong.

RESPONSE TO SPECIFIC BIBLICAL ARGUMENTS FOR REINCARNATION

While those who hold to reincarnation sometimes quote the Bible to support their doctrine we find that the Scriptures cited do not mean anything like what reincarnationists says they do. Indeed, the Bible makes it clear that, once a person has died, there is no possibility to return in another human form. Consequently, Scripture refutes the arguments for reincarnation. Let's now examine the evidence.

HUMANS HAVE NO KNOWLEDGE BEFORE BIRTH

Contrary to what reincarnation teaches, humans have no knowledge before birth. While the Bible says that God knew us before we were born, there is nothing in Scripture that says that we knew anything. The example of God knowing the prophet Jeremiah does not support the doctrine of reincarnation. The Bible says that God ordained Jeremiah to the work of the ministry before he was born, nothing more. Before he was born, God knew Jeremiah but Jeremiah did not know God. Jeremiah, like the rest of us, knew nothing!

THERE IS NO PREEXISTENT STATE FOR HUMANS

There is something else. Nowhere does the Bible teach that there is some sort of a preexistent state for humans. Humans have no existence until they are conceived, none whatsoever. We do not exist previously to our conception in the womb.

ELIJAH WAS NOT JOHN THE BAPTIST

John the Baptist could not have been the reincarnation of Elijah as reincarnationists teach. They were two distinct people. There are a number of reasons as to why this is so.

For one thing, the Old Testament says that Elijah himself was to come to earth before the great and terrible day of the Lord. We read the words of the Lord through the prophet Malachi.

> See, I am sending my messenger to prepare the way before me, and the Lord whom you seek will suddenly come to his temple. The messenger of the covenant in whom you deligh—indeed, he is coming, says the LORD of hosts.... Lo, I will send you the prophet Elijah before the great and terrible day of the LORD comes. He will turn the hearts of parents to their children and the hearts of children to their parents, so that I will not come and strike the land with a curse (Malachi 3:1; 4:5-6 NRSV).

Elijah is personally going to come before the great and terrible day of the Lord.

John's birth was foretold by the angel Gabriel to his father Zechariah. We read about who his exact identity.

> And he will go on before the Lord, in the spirit and power of Elijah, to turn the hearts of the fathers to their children and the disobedient to the wisdom of the righteous—to make ready a people prepared for the Lord (Luke 1:17 NIV).

Here we are specifically told that John would come in the spirit and power of Elijah, not that he would actually be Elijah. John had a similar ministry to Elijah in that he attempted to turn the hearts of a sinful nation back to the Lord.

In addition, when he was directly asked, John the Baptist said that he was not Elijah. We read the following in John's gospel.

> And they asked him, "What then? Are you Elijah?" He said, "I am not." "Are you the Prophet?" And he answered, "No" (John 1:21 ESV).

John said that he was not Elijah. This should settle the matter.

The Bible also says Elijah appeared with Moses at the transfiguration of Jesus. Scripture records it this way.

> After six days Jesus took with him Peter, James and John the brother of James, and led them up a high mountain by themselves. There he was transfigured before them. His face shone like the sun, and his clothes became as white as the light. Just then there appeared before them Moses and Elijah, talking with Jesus (Matthew 17:1-3 NIV).

There is no indication that Elijah was somehow identified with John the Baptist when he appeared with Moses. Elijah was Elijah and John the Baptist was John the Baptist. The two are never confused.

Furthermore, Elijah did not die! If Elijah did not die, then he certainly could not have been reincarnated. The Bible says the following happened to him.

> As they were walking along and talking, suddenly a chariot of fire appeared, drawn by horses of fire. It drove between them, separating them, and Elijah was carried by a whirlwind into heaven (2 Kings 2:11 NLT).

Elijah was not the same person as John the Baptist. They are different people.

Therefore, when Jesus said Elijah had already come, His disciples realized that He was speaking about John the Baptist. Therefore, we should not assume that John was literally Elijah. John came to fulfill the role of Elijah. Elijah will indeed come in the future but John was not him.

There are two comings of Christ. At the First Coming an Elijah-like character appeared, John the Baptist. At the Second Coming, Elijah himself will appear. Most likely, he is one of the two witnesses spoken of in Revelation 11.

BORN AGAIN MEANS BORN FROM ABOVE

The fact that Jesus told Nicodemus must be "born again" was not a reference to him coming back in another life as another person. There are a couple of things which should be noted. The words "born again" can be translated "born from above." It was not another physical birth which Nicodemus needed but rather a "new birth," a spiritual rebirth.

Nicodemus did not have any concept of reincarnation as being a possible option. His response to Jesus' shows this. He said.

> "How can a man be born when he is old?" Nicodemus asked.
> "Surely he cannot enter a second time into his mother's
> womb to be born!" (John 3:4 NIV).

The way Nicodemus responded to Jesus shows that he did not consider reincarnation as a possibility. Jesus then went on to tell Nicodemus that it was a spiritual rebirth which he and all the other people of Israel needed.

This idea of being "born again" is later spoken of by Peter. He wrote

> For you have been born again, not of perishable seed, but of
> imperishable, through the living and enduring word of God
> (1 Peter 1:23 NIV).

The people to whom Peter wrote were already "born again." They did not have to die physically to attain this. Thus, being "born again" is another way of describing belief in Jesus. Born again is a spiritual rebirth.

THE BELIEF OF JESUS' DISCIPLES ABOUT THE MAN BORN BLIND IS NOT RELEVANT

Often it is argued that Jesus' disciples believed in some sort of reincarnation, or previous existence of the soul, because they asked Him a question about a man who had been born blind. They wanted to know if the blind man had sinned or if his parents had sinned to cause him to be born without sight. The question seems to indicate that they believed in some type of pre-existence of the soul or reincarnation. Otherwise how could he have sinned before his birth?

Whether or not Jesus' disciples believed in some sort of pre-existence of the soul is not the real issue. Indeed, they are not the final authority. It is only the words of Jesus that have any authority and He did not teach that the soul had any type of existence before a person is conceived.

We also know that there was no belief in reincarnation among the Jews at the time of Christ. However, there were some Jewish teachings which did believe in some type of preexistence of the souls of the unborn.

Yet it is not likely that the disciples had this in mind. Rather they probably wondered if the man may have sinned while he was still in the womb. This was a popular Jewish belief at the time of Jesus. It assumed that birth defects could come from either sin by the baby in the womb or by sins of relatives of the unborn. These sins would cause their offspring some physical problem.

Whatever the case may be, we should not assume that Jesus' disciples believed in some type of reincarnation when they asked Him whether or not this man's blindness was caused by his sin previous to birth.

MELCHIZEDEK DID HAVE A BEGINNING

The New Testament does not say that Melchizedek did not have a beginning or end as is alleged by those who believe in reincarnation. It merely says that what we know about him from the Old Testament is limited. We are not told the names of his mother or father or his ancestors. However, this does not mean that he had no father, mother or ancestors. Melchizedek is an illustration of Jesus insofar as he had no beginning or end as far as Scripture is concerned. Jesus had no beginning because He is the eternal God who became a human being. Melchizedek is not an illustration of reincarnation.

THERE IS NO WHEEL IN THE SENSE OF REINCARNATION'S ENDLESS REBIRTHS

The reference to James and the wheel of life is misleading. It does not refer to the wheel or cycle of endless rebirths as taught by reincarnationists but rather it speaks of the entire course of ones life. Modern translations make this clear. The English Standard Version says.

> And the tongue is a fire, a world of unrighteousness. The tongue is set among our members, staining the whole body, setting on fire the entire course of life, and set on fire by hell (James 3:6 ESV).

This clearer translation of the words of James demonstrates that he did not have reincarnation in mind when he wrote.

THE LAW OF CAUSE AND EFFECT IS TRUE BUT NOT IN THE SENSE OF REINCARNATION

A number of passages used by those who believe in reincarnation speak of the law of cause and effect. However, they are not to be understood in the same sense as those who believe in reincarnation.

In fact, Galatians 6:7, which is often cited by reincarnationists, is only partially quoted. It says the following in context.

Do not be deceived: God cannot be mocked. A man reaps
what he sows. The one who sows to please his sinful nature,
from that nature will reap destruction; the one who sows
to please the Spirit, from the Spirit will reap eternal life
(Galatians 6:7-8 NIV).

To begin with, we must understand that this verse assumes that a personal God exists. This is contrary to the belief of reincarnation. Next
we are told that those who sow to the spirit reap eternal life but those
who sow to the flesh reap destruction. Destruction refers to eternal
separation from God, the judgment of hell. Again, this is something
reincarnation does not teach. Nothing in this passage suggests that the
human spirit is reincarnated in another life as a different person.

Other passages which supposedly refer to the law of cause and effect
in the sense of karma do no such thing. Again, the law of karma is not
taught in Scripture.

RESURRECTION IS NOT REINCARNATION

Scripture teaches resurrection, not reincarnation. Resurrection means
restoration in our present bodies. Jesus rose with the same body that was
put into the tomb. This was His own testimony as to what occurred.
We read in John's gospel.

So the Jews replied to Him, "What sign [of authority]
will You show us for doing these things?" Jesus answered,
"Destroy this sanctuary, and I will raise it up in three days."
Therefore the Jews said, "This sanctuary took 46 years to
build, and will You raise it up in three days?" But He was
speaking about the sanctuary of His body. So when He was
raised from the dead, His disciples remembered that He had
said this. And they believed the Scripture and the statement
Jesus had made (John 2:18-22 HCSB).

It was His body that was to be raised from the dead.

On the day of His resurrection, Jesus said.

> See my hands and my feet, that it is I myself. Touch me, and
> see. For a spirit does not have flesh and bones as you see that
> I have (Luke 24:39 ESV).

Jesus came back in a resurrected body but it was the same Jesus.

John wrote about Jesus telling Thomas to touch His body. We read the
following in the Gospel of John.

> Then he said to Thomas, "Put your finger here and see my
> hands. Reach out your hand and put it in my side. Do not
> doubt but believe" (John 20:27 NRSV).

Reincarnation says we come back to this world in another body as
a different person. Resurrection, not reincarnation is what the Bible
promises. The word resurrection is found often in Scripture. It is used
of the dead body of Jesus which was raised to life. In Jesus' case, raised
in a body that would never again die, a glorified body.

However, the word reincarnation is never found in the Bible nor is any
similar word. Reincarnation is simply not taught in Scripture.

The evidence shows that passages used by reincarnationists are misap-
plied and used out of context. Consequently, there is no biblical evidence for the doctrine of reincarnation. None whatsoever.

WHAT THE BIBLE DOES TEACH ABOUT THESE SUBJECTS?

So far we have seen what the Bible does not teach. Now we want to
consider some of the things it does teach about salvation, judgment
and related subjects.

1. AFTER DEATH THERE IS JUDGMENT

The Bible says that after death comes judgment. There is no coming
back to live another life as another person. The writer to the Hebrews
stated it this way.

And just as it is appointed for man to die once, and after that comes judgment (Hebrews 9:27 ESV).

Judgment comes after death, not another chance at life in another human form. We must face the consequences of how we have lived in this life after we die. There are no second chances, no ability to make any more decisions. Destines have been determined once and for all.

2. JESUS WAS THE SACRIFICIAL LAMB

This brings us to one of the main points of Scripture. Jesus Christ came into the world to be a sacrifice for sin. Indeed, Jesus' death on the cross is what takes the sins of the world away. John the Baptist testified to Him as follows.

The next day he saw Jesus coming toward him and declared, "Here is the Lamb of God who takes away the sin of the world" (John 1:29 NRSV).

Jesus died as the "lamb of God" for the sins of the world. His sacrifice is what saves us. We cannot take away our own sin by self-effort

3. THE DEATH OF CHRIST IS SUFFICIENT FOR SIN

Those who hold a belief in reincarnation deny the worth of the death of Jesus Christ. Yet the Bible teaches that Christ's death satisfied God's standards.

It's the same way with the Son of Man. He didn't come so that others could serve him. He came to serve and to give his life as a ransom for many people (Matthew 20:28 God's Word).

His death is satisfactory to save us from sin. Nothing else is necessary.

4. HE REDEEMED US WITH HIS BLOOD

Salvation is accomplished by His death on the cross, not our own good works. Paul said the following to the elders at the church in Ephesus.

> Therefore take heed to yourselves and to all the flock, among which the Holy Spirit has made you overseers, to shepherd the church of God which He purchased with His own blood (Acts 20:28 NKJV).

Jesus redeemed us with His blood. He has paid the price for our sins. We have no ability whatsoever to pay for our own sins.

5. JESUS BORE THE CURSE FOR ALL HUMANITY

The Bible says that Jesus Christ suffered on behalf of us so that we do not have to suffer ourselves. He became a curse for us. Paul wrote.

> Christ redeemed us from the curse of the law by becoming a curse for us—for it is written, "Cursed is everyone who hangs on a tree" (Galatians 3:13 NRSV).

Jesus took the curse, the condemnation, which we deserved.

6. JESUS TOOK OUR SIN ON HIMSELF

The Bible says Christ bore our sin on the cross. The Book of Hebrews emphasizes that Jesus sacrificed Himself on our behalf.

> For it was fitting that we should have such a high priest, holy, blameless, undefiled, separated from sinners, and exalted above the heavens. Unlike the other high priests, he has no need to offer sacrifices day after day, first for his own sins, and then for those of the people; this he did once for all when he offered himself (Hebrews 7:26,27 NRSV).

His sacrifice paid the price for our sins. In other words, we do not have to pay for them with our own good works. This is the good news of the gospel.

7. THE HOPE FOR BELIEVERS IS THE REDEMPTION OR TRANSFORMATION OF OUR BODY

The hope for the believer is the redemption, the transformation, of our individual body. Paul wrote.

> And we believers also groan, even though we have the Holy Spirit within us as a foretaste of future glory, for we long for our bodies to be released from sin and suffering. We, too, wait with eager hope for the day when God will give us our full rights as his adopted children, including the new bodies he has promised us (Romans 8:23 NLT).

It is the one body (singular) which is to be redeemed, not many bodies which we have had throughout history. Indeed, it is our present body which will be transformed.

Paul wrote to the Philippians about how Christ will change our mortal bodies to bodies like His. He put it this way.

> But our citizenship is in heaven, from which we also eagerly wait for a Savior, the Lord Jesus Christ. He will transform the body of our humble condition into the likeness of His glorious body, by the power that enables Him to subject everything to Himself (Philippians 3:20-21 HCSB).

The new body will have continuity with our present body. Paul explained this as he wrote the following to the Corinthians.

> So it is with the resurrection of the dead: Sown in corruption, raised in incorruption; sown in dishonor, raised in glory; sown in weakness, raised in power; sown a natural body, raised a spiritual body. If there is a natural body, there is also a spiritual body (1 Corinthians 15:42-44 HCSB).

It is the same body because we are the same person.

8. WE DO NOT WORK FOR OUR SALVATION

Humans do not earn salvation. Our works, not matter how good they may be, cannot please God. The Bible tells us God's view of our works.

> All of us have become like something unclean, and all our righteous acts are like a polluted garment; all of us wither like a leaf, and our iniquities carry us away like the wind (Isaiah 64:6 HCSB).

Our works do not bring spiritual life. They cannot take away our sin.

If one wishes to do the works of God, then they must believe in Jesus Christ. Jesus Himself made this plain. We read in John.

> "What can we do to perform the works of God?" they asked. Jesus replied, "This is the work of God: that you believe in the One He has sent" (John 6:28,29 HCSB).

Believing in Jesus is the work of God; it is not earning eternal life by our own good works. Reincarnation, on the other hand, appeals to the pride of human beings. We earn our own salvation. Our own efforts merit some type of a reward. This is in total contrast to the gospel message which says we cannot do it on our own. Our destiny is not determined by our own set of good works.

9. BELIEVER'S IMMEDIATELY GO TO BE WITH THE LORD

Those who die do not come back again to the earth as another person. Indeed, those who have believed in Christ go to be with the Lord immediately.

Paul wrote the following to the Corinthians about this wonderful truth.

> Yes, we are of good courage, and we would rather be away from the body and at home with the Lord (2 Corinthians 5:8 ESV).

The believing dead go to be immediately with the Lord and the unbelieving dead go to a place apart from Him. There is no third place for anyone to go. Certainly, they do not go into another body.

10. SALVATION BECOMES IMMEDIATE FOR THE BELIEVER

The Bible says that "now" is the time of salvation, it is immediate. We read in Second Corinthians the following words of Paul.

> For God says, "At just the right time, I heard you. On the day of salvation, I helped you." Indeed, God is ready to help you right now. Today is the day of salvation (2 Corinthians 6:2 NLT).

Salvation is now; not in some future life.

11. WE LEAVE THIS WORLD WITH NOTHING

Contrary to the teaching of reincarnation, the Bible says we leave the world with nothing. In the Book of Job, we note the following.

> Job stood up and tore his robe in grief. Then he shaved his head and fell to the ground to worship. He said, "I came naked from my mother's womb, and I will be naked when I leave. The Lord gave me what I had, and the Lord has taken it away. Praise the name of the Lord (Job 1:20,21 NLT).

Just as we cannot bring anything with us when we come into this world, we cannot take anything with us from this world when we leave it.

CONCLUSION: THERE IS NO COMING BACK FROM THE DEAD AS REINCARNATION TEACHES

It is not possible for humans to come back to earth in another form. This includes as either another human being or some other form of plant or animal life. The Western idea of reincarnation, coming back as another human, or the Eastern idea of transmigration of souls, coming back as a human, plant, or animal, is not biblical. Once a person dies there is no coming back. The belief in reincarnation is based upon human speculation of what occurs, it is not based upon divine revelation.

SUMMARY TO QUESTION 30
DO HUMAN COME BACK IN OTHER LIVES AS DIFFERENT PEOPLE (REINCARNATION) WHAT DOES THE BIBLE SAY ABOUT THIS SUBJECT?

The doctrine of reincarnation states that this life is not all that there is for us. It is argued that each of us may have been someone else in a past life where we lived as another person, in another place, and at a different time.

Furthermore, we may come back to this earth as another person sometime in the future. Consequently we may be someone else in our next life. The reason this occurs is because we are working out our own salvation. Until our character, and our behavior, reaches a certain degree of perfection, where we no longer have to live on this earth, we will continue to return as different human beings.

Scripture as well as personal experience are appealed to in advocating the doctrine of reincarnation.

However the doctrine of reincarnation is not taught in Scripture. To begin with, the Bible knows nothing of any preexistent state of humans where we have knowledge before our birth. According to Scripture, we do not exist until we are conceived in the womb. The doctrine of the preexistence of souls is not a biblical doctrine.

Neither does the Bible say that Elijah was John the Baptist as reincarnationists claim. John himself said he was not Elijah. John came in a ministry similar to that of Elijah, warning the people of the coming judgment unless they repented.

The question that Jesus' disciples asked about a man born blind does not mean they believed in reincarnation. It was a popular belief at the time of Jesus that there could be sin in the womb which would cause physical defects upon birth. Furthermore, it does not matter what the disciples said or believed. The issue is what Jesus Christ taught. He did not believe in reincarnation.

Contrary to the teaching of reincarnation, the Old Testament character Melchizedek did have a beginning but it is not recorded in the Old Testament. This is why he is similar to Christ; he had no recorded beginning. Melchizedek is not an example of reincarnation.

In addition, after death, the Bible says there is only judgment, there is no second chance. This is because Jesus Christ paid the price once and for all for the sins of the world. Thus, it is not necessary for us to pay for our sins. Scripture says that the death of Christ was sufficient. The Bible says that He took our suffering upon Himself. We cannot pay for our own sins no matter how much we may suffer.

In fact, we cannot do any good deeds in order to please God. As far as obtaining eternal salvation is concerned, our works are worthless. The only work we can do is to believe in Him whom He has sent. Salvation from sin is a gift. It is not something which is earned.

When a person believes in Jesus Christ, salvation becomes immediate. The person is then "born again." They have a spiritual rebirth. Born again, therefore, means being, "born from above." It does not refer a succession of births in this world.

Moreover, Scripture teaches resurrection not reincarnation. Indeed, Jesus rose with the same body that was put into the tomb. He did not have a different body when He came back to life three days after He was dead. Hence, His resurrection cannot be used as an example of reincarnation or coming back in a different form as a different person. Indeed, He was the same person before and after His death.

It becomes obvious that reincarnation, when weighed by the balances of the Word of God, is found wanting.

QUESTION 31

Were Texts Which Support Reincarnation Removed From The Bible?

While reincarnationists often appeal to the Bible to support their belief system, some of them actually claim that texts in Scripture which support the idea of reincarnation were removed by the church. Supposedly, at some time in the past, these passages were excised from the Bible by church authorities to cover up the fact that the Bible taught reincarnation.

Is there any evidence of this? Has the text of Scripture been tampered for the purpose of removing references to reincarnation? We can make the following observations.

THIS IS AN INCONSISTENT POSITION BY REINCARNATIONISTS

Reincarnationists are inconsistent when they claim certain texts were removed from Scripture which support their belief system. For one thing, they point to a number of passages which are presently in the Bible which they claim give evidence of the belief of the biblical writers in reincarnation. Therefore, if the church authorities removed certain texts from Scripture that supported reincarnation, they were rather incompetent in their removal because, according to reincarnationists, other texts still exist which teach their doctrine!

REINCARNATION WAS NEVER AN ISSUE

The claim that texts were removed has no merit whatsoever. Indeed, there is no evidence that the doctrine of reincarnation was ever discussed by church officials as a viable option at any time in church history. In other words, it was never an issue.

The only subject that was discussed, which is even remotely related, is the subject of the pre-existence of souls. The belief in the pre-existence of the soul was held by an early church father named Origen. Origen was condemned by the church leaders for his heretical or non-biblical view. However, Origen made it clear that he did not believe in the idea of reincarnation. Other early theologians explicitly rejected any idea of reincarnation because they believed and taught that it was contrary to Scripture. Therefore, it was never a debatable issue among Bible-believers.

THERE IS NO HISTORICAL BASIS FOR THIS CLAIM

When the historical evidence is examined we find no basis for the claim that certain texts were removed from Scripture which supported reincarnation. The text of Scripture reads the same as it was originally written. This has been demonstrated over and over again. What we read today in both testaments faithfully represents what was originally written by the authors of Scripture.

Consequently, there is no factual basis for the contention that certain texts have been removed from the Bible because they supported the idea of reincarnation.

SUMMARY TO QUESTION 31
WERE TEXTS WHICH SUPPORT REINCARNATION REMOVED FROM THE BIBLE?

The accusation is sometimes made by those who believe in the doctrine of reincarnation that certain texts which support their belief have been removed from Scripture.

This removal supposedly came after the time of Jesus Christ by church authorities who wanted to hide the true belief of the biblical writers.

While reincarnation was originally taught, there was the attempt to remove all aspects of it from the Scripture.

However, this claim has no basis in fact. Indeed, those who advocate this position have a number of questions to answer.

For one thing, those who accept reincarnation as true often cite a number of biblical passages as supportive of their claims. If there are passages in Scripture which support reincarnation, as they claim that there are, then how can it logically be claimed that other passages were removed? When were they removed and who removed them? Reincarnationists have no answer because there is no answer. Texts were not removed.

Neither do we find that reincarnation was a topic of discussion among early church leaders. Indeed, it was not an issue for them.

Furthermore, why didn't these authorities remove all references to reincarnation, not merely some? Those who promote this position have no answer. No proof is offered nor can it be offered because there is no evidence that this ever occurred.

As we examine how the text has been transmitted to us we find that it says the same thing as what was originally written. It hasn't been changed or altered. The same message is found in every text, every manuscript. This message of the Bible does not include the doctrine of reincarnation.

Consequently, we conclude that no texts were removed from either testament which supports the false teaching of reincarnation. None.

What Observations And Conclusions Can We Make About What Happens To Us One Second After We Die?

In this book we have looked at the subject of the intermediate or in-between state of the dead; what happens immediately after we die. We discovered that this is a temporary state of humans between this life and our eventual resurrection from the dead and the final judgment. In other words, it is not our ultimate destination.

From Scripture, we can make a number of observations and conclusions with respect to the in-between state. They are as follows.

OBSERVATION 1: THERE ARE LIMITED THINGS REVEALED

To begin with, Scripture does not reveal very many things about the temporary state of the dead. Indeed, it is much more interested in our eternal state; where all of us will eventually end up. Therefore, the information we do have is limited.

OBSERVATION 2: WE CAN KNOW CERTAIN THINGS

Even though the information on the in-between state of the dead is fragmentary, there are still a number of things which we can learn from the Scripture. Therefore, we are not completely ignorant about what happens to people immediately upon death.

OBSERVATION 3: THERE IS A TEMPORARY STATE OF THE DEAD

It is clear that death does not bring us to our final destination. Instead there is a temporary state before the resurrection of the dead and then the final judgment. Therefore, our lives are in three stages; the time we spend here upon earth, then the time in the intermediate state, and finally there is eternity.

OBSERVATION 4: THOSE WHO HAVE DIED ARE CONSCIOUS IN THE IN-BETWEEN STATE

The dead are not asleep in the grave as some people like to think. The bodies are in the grave but the spirits are alive and conscious. Believers are in a state of complete happiness and bliss in the presence of the Lord while unbelievers are suffering while waiting for their final judgment.

OBSERVATION 5: THE INTERMEDIATE STATE IS AN INCOMPLETE STATE

We also learned that the intermediate state of the dead is an incomplete state. While the Bible represents it as conscious joy for the believer and conscious pain for the unbeliever, it also represents it a state that is incomplete. Indeed, the perfect joy of the believers and the ultimate misery of the unbelievers will only begin with the resurrection from the dead and the final judgment.

OBSERVATION 6: THIS TEMPORARY STATE WILL END SOMEDAY

Since the in-between state is only for a limited period of time, it will eventually end. In fact, Scripture says that both death and the temporary realm of the dead, Hades, will be thrown into the lake of fire. In other words, they will cease to exist.

OBSERVATION 7: OUR DESTINIES ARE DETERMINED DURING OUR LIFETIME

It is crucial for us to realize that where we will spend eternity is determined in this life; not in the in-between state. Indeed, eternal destinies have already been determined the moment we enter the afterlife. There is no second chance, no coming back. This life determines what will happen in the next. Indeed, once we reach the "other side" our future has been settled.

A FINAL QUESTION

With these things in mind, the question each of us has to answer is this: when this life is over will you be in the presence of the Lord or forever banished from His presence? The choice is yours.

SUMMARY TO QUESTION 32
WHAT OBSERVATIONS AND CONCLUSIONS CAN WE MAKE ABOUT WHAT HAPPENS TO US ONE SECOND AFTER WE DIE?

From a study of the Scripture we can make a number of conclusions about the in-between or intermediate state of the dead.

To begin with, though the Bible does not give us much information on what happens immediately after we die, it does tell us certain things.

What we do know is this: there is a temporary state of the dead which everyone enters immediately upon their death. This occurs before the resurrection of the dead and the final judgments on the human race.

We also know that those who have died are conscious. They are either in the presence of the Lord or they are separated from Him. Because the intermediate state is temporary it means it is incomplete. While the believers are in a state of joy and bliss, and the unbelievers in a state of misery, the complete joy for the believer and the fullness of the punishment for the unbeliever will take place in the future.

The temporary state will end someday and then eternity will begin. However, destinies will have already been decided in this life and in it alone. Therefore, once a person enters the in-between state their eternal destiny has been forever settled.

Consequently, it is crucial that unbelievers make their decision for Jesus Christ while they still have the chance. Indeed, once this life is over there is no possibility to change our eternal destination. There is no second chance, no hope for the unbelieving dead. That's the bad news.

The good news is that there is still hope for the living. Hopefully, everyone who is reading this has made his or her personal decision for Christ. If so, you can be confident in the knowledge about what awaits you once this life is over.

APPENDIX 1

What Are The Various
Views Of Sheol

The Hebrew word "Sheol" is used 65 times in the Old Testament. Though it is often translated "hell" in the some of the older English versions, this gives the wrong inference. It is never used of the final destination of the wicked. The following are some of the ways in which Bible-believers interpret the word Sheol.

1. THE GRAVE-THE ACTUAL PLACE WHERE BODIES ARE BURIED

2. THE UNSEEN REALM OF THE DEAD-THE UNDERWORLD

3. SPECIFICALLY, THE PLACE OF PUNISHMENT FOR THE WICKED

4. IT IS USED SYMBOLICALLY

5. IT SPEAKS OF THE PLACE FROM WHERE THE RIGHTEOUS ARE SAVED

These are the various ways in which the Old Testament uses this term. However, there is disagreement at to whether certain of these interpretations are to be understood in a literal manner.

Many Bible students see only "one meaning" of Sheol, the grave. In other words, it only refers to the place where the dead are buried. The other meanings are found in poetical contexts and are not be understood literally.

THE CONTEXT DETERMINES THE MEANING OF SHEOL

Even if we are to assume each of these five meaning can be attached to the word Sheol, at times, it is difficult to know which of these categories Sheol is referring to. In other words, the exact meaning is hard to determine. In fact, it can overlap these categories. Consequently it is essential to check out the context to find the correct meaning of Sheol each time it is used.

THE USES OF SHEOL IN THE OLD TESTAMENT

We will now consider the different ways in which Sheol is used in the Old Testament. They are as follows.

1. SHEOL REPRESENTS THE GRAVE

The primary meaning of Sheol seems to be the actual physical place where the literal bodies of the dead are buried. The psalmist wrote.

> Like a rock that one breaks apart and shatters on the land,
> so shall their bones be strewn at the mouth of Sheol (Psalm 141:7 NRSV).

The New International Version translates Sheol as "the grave" in this context.

> *They will say*, "As one plows and breaks up the earth, so our bones have been scattered at the mouth of the grave" (Psalm 141:7 NIV).

This use of the word refers to the actual place the bodies are placed once a person dies, namely the grave.

The patriarch Jacob was sorrowful at what he thought was the loss of his youngest son Benjamin. He put it this way.

> But he said, "My son shall not go down with you, for his brother is dead, and he is the only one left. If harm should

happen to him on the journey that you are to make, you would bring down my gray hairs with sorrow to Sheol (Genesis 42:38 ESV).

In this instance, Sheol could refer either to the actual grave or merely the realm of the dead. As we indicated, some see an overlap between the various meanings of the word.

2. SHEOL IS THE UNSEEN REALM OF THE DEAD

As mentioned, it is argued that Sheol can mean the unseen realm of the dead, the present state of the deceased. Both the godly and ungodly go to Sheol in this sense of the term. When used in this way, there is no idea of a place of judgment or condemnation.

It is, for example, the place where the righteous Jacob would go. We read of this in Genesis. It says.

> All his sons and all his daughters sought to comfort him; but he refused to be comforted, and said, "No, I shall go down to Sheol to my son, mourning." Thus his father bewailed him (Genesis 37:35 NRSV).

Some contend that Jacob was indicating that he was going to go to realm of the dead, the place in the unseen world where spirits of the dead gather. However, his statement could merely mean that he was going to the grave, nothing more.

Sheol was also the place where sinners would end up once they passed on. We read the following in the Book of Numbers.

> But if the Lord creates something new, and the ground opens its mouth and swallows them up with all that belongs to them, and they go down alive into Sheol, then you shall know that these men have despised the Lord (Numbers 16:30 ESV).

The New Living Translation translates the verse in this manner.

> But if the LORD performs a miracle and the ground opens
> up and swallows them and all their belongings, and they go
> down alive into the grave, then you will know that these men
> have despised the LORD (Numbers 16:30 NLT).

In this context, Sheol may have the idea of the living going to the place where the dead reside. Yet it is also possible it is only referring to the grave and not the place of departed spirits.

Consequently, these passages may simply be referring to the grave, the actual burial place of the dead, and nothing more.

3. IT IS THE PLACE OF PUNISHMENT FOR THE WICKED

While Sheol originally meant only the grave, it seems that the word eventually came to be used of the temporary place of punishment for the wicked. In other words, Sheol is the place where the deceased unbelievers are gathered while awaiting God's coming judgment.

IT IS THE PLACE OF SPIRITUAL DEATH

Therefore, the word Sheol can be refer to a place in the unseen realm of spiritual death, or spiritual separation from God. We read the following in the Book of Psalms.

> Let death come upon them; let them go down alive to Sheol; for
> evil is in their homes and in their hearts (Psalm 55:15 NRSV).

Those who are spiritually dead, the wicked, are punished in Sheol. In Sheol, they await the final judgment. Yet again, this may be reading too much into this particular passage.

SHEOL HAS AN INSATIABLE APPETITE FOR THE WICKED

We are told that Sheol has an appetite that cannot be satisfied. We read about this in the Book of Proverbs. It says.

Death and the grave [*sheol*] are never satisfied, and neither are we (Proverbs 27:20 God's Word).

We also read in Proverbs.

The leech has two daughters: Give and Give. Three things are never satisfied; four never say, "Enough": Sheol, the barren womb, the land never satisfied with water, and the fire that never says, "Enough (Proverbs 30:15,16 ESV).

Sheol is never satisfied.

The prophet Isaiah also wrote of the appetite of Sheol.

Therefore Sheol has enlarged its appetite and opened its mouth beyond measure; the nobility of Jerusalem and her multitude go down, her throng and all who exult in her (Isaiah 5:14 NRSV).

The prophet Habakkuk spoke of the width of Sheol.

Moreover, wealth is treacherous; the arrogant do not endure. They open their throats wide as Sheol; like Death they never have enough. They gather all nations for themselves, and collect all peoples as their own (Habakkuk 2:5 NRSV).

Sheol is thus spoken of as never being able to be satisfied. It has an insatiable appetite. Again, while this may only be referring to the grave, the place of burial, it also may also be referring to the temporary place of punishment for the wicked.

4. SHEOL IS USED SYMBOLICALLY

Sheol is also used symbolically in the Old Testament. We find the following examples of this use of the term.

A. IT IS SYMBOLIC FOR GREAT SIN

We find Sheol used symbolically for great sin. The prophet Isaiah wrote.

> Because you have said, "We have made a covenant with death and with Sheol we have an agreement, when the overwhelming whip passes through it will not come to us, for we have made lies our refuge, and in falsehood we have taken shelter" (Isaiah 28:15 ESV).

Sheol and sin are seemingly used interchangeably in this passage.

B. IT IS SYMBOLIC FOR GREED

Sheol is also used symbolically for greed. The prophet Habakkuk wrote.

> Indeed, wine betrays him; he is arrogant and never at rest. Because he is as greedy as the grave and like death is never satisfied, he gathers to himself all the nations and takes captive all the peoples (Habakkuk 2:5 NIV).

Sheol is equated with greed.

5. IT IS THE PLACE FROM WHICH THE RIGHTEOUS ARE SAVED

While the wicked remain in Sheol, it is the place from where the righteous are saved. The psalmist wrote about God saving people from the power of Sheol. He put it this way.

> But God will ransom my soul from the power of Sheol, for he will receive me (Psalm 49:15 NRSV).

The psalmist also wrote.

> For great is your steadfast love toward me; you have delivered my soul from the depths of Sheol (Psalm 86:13 ESV).

The righteous are saved from Sheol.

These passages may be speaking of only death itself rather than a specific place the departed spirits go to. However, the second part of Psalm 49:15 "he will receive me" is seen by many to indicate conscious existence after this life is over.

SOME FURTHER OBSERVATIONS ABOUT SHEOL

There are a number of other observations we can make about Sheol from the Old Testament. They are as follows.

1. SHEOL IS STILL WITHIN GOD'S REACH

Those in Sheol, though they may be dead, are still within the reach of the God of the Bible. The prophet Amos said.

> If they dig into Sheol, from there shall my hand take them; if they climb up to heaven, from there I will bring them down (Amos 9:2 ESV).

Like everything else in the universe, Sheol can be reached by the God of Scripture.

Sheol has no lasting influence on the godly. We read in Hosea.

> Shall I ransom them from the power of Sheol? Shall I redeem them from Death? O Death, where are your plagues? O Sheol, where is your destruction? Compassion is hidden from my eyes (Hosea 13:14 NRSV).

Sheol here seems to be synonymous with death. The good news is that Sheol has only temporary influence on the godly. It will have no lasting influence on those who belong to the Lord.

2. SHEOL IS SYMBOLICALLY LOCATED IN THE LOWER PARTS OF THE EARTH

Whenever there is a geographic reference to Sheol, it is described as being below, in the lower parts of the earth. God said.

> For a fire is kindled by my anger, and it burns to the depths of Sheol, devours the earth and its increase, and sets on fire the foundations of the mountains (Deuteronomy 32:22 ESV).

This of course, is only a symbolic description.

3. SHEOL IS CONTRASTED WITH THE HIGHEST HEAVEN

In the Book of Job, Sheol is contrasted with the highest heaven. It says.

> It is higher than heaven—what can you do? Deeper than Sheol—what can you know (Job 11:8 ESV).

The New Living Translation says.

> Such knowledge is higher than the heavens—but who are you? It is deeper than the underworld—what can you know in comparison to him? (Job 11:8 NLT).

Sheol is deeper than the underworld.

In the Book of Proverbs it says the following about Sheol being a place which is below.

> For the wise the path of life leads upward, in order to avoid Sheol below (Proverbs 15:24 NRSV).

The Contemporary English Version translates it this way.

> All who are wise follow a road that leads upward to life and away from death (Proverbs 15:24 CEV).

The direction of life is upward while the direction of death or Sheol is downward.

4. IT IS THE LOWEST DEPTHS

Sheol is not only located downward, it is in the lowest depths. Isaiah the prophet said.

Yet you shall be brought down to Sheol, to the lowest depths of the Pit (Isaiah 14:15 NKJV).

The New Living Translation says.

But instead, you will be brought down to the place of the dead, down to its lowest depths (Isaiah 14:15 NLT).

Ezekiel testified that Sheol is located in a downward direction. He explained it in this manner.

They also went down to Sheol with it, to those who are slain by the sword; yes, those who were its arm, who lived under its shadow among the nations (Ezekiel 31:17 ESV).

Since every geographic description of Sheol refers to some place that is down, it has led some theologians to suggest that Sheol is somewhere in the heart of the earth.

5. IT IS NOT THE FINAL STATE OF THE RIGHTEOUS

Whatever the term Sheol means, it is clear it was never regarded as the ultimate home of the righteous. It was, at best, only a temporary place where the righteous dead went when they died. However, God has promised them something better.

6. THE WICKED WILL EVENTUALLY LEAVE SHEOL

Sheol is also a temporary place for the wicked dead. After the resurrection and final judgment of all humanity, the wicked will be sent to their ultimate destination, Gehenna. This is also known as "hell" or the "lake of fire."

We read about this in the Book of Revelation where it tells us that Sheol, or Hades, will no longer exist.

Then Death and Hades were thrown into the lake of fire. This is the second death, the lake of fire (Revelation 20:14 ESV).

Sheol, then, is seen as a temporary place of the departed. It will eventually be destroyed when the Lord creates a new heaven and a new earth.

SUMMARY TO APPENDIX 1
WHAT ARE THE VARIOUS VIEWS OF SHEOL

According to the Old Testament, all people who die go to "Sheol." This Hebrew word, unfortunately translated "hell" in some English versions, has a variety of meanings and these meanings must be determined by the context.

The main meaning of the word is "the grave." It is the place where the bodies of the dead are buried. Everyone agrees upon this. However, there is no agreement among Bible students upon other possible meanings of Sheol. Indeed, many assume that the grave is the "only" meaning of this Hebrew word.

Where it does speak of the souls of the departed spirits it is always in a poetic context. Consequently, many believe that Sheol is not meant to be literally understood as a place where the spirits of the dead congregate.

Some argue that while the word originally meant the grave, it later took on the meaning of the place in the netherworld where the spirits of the deceased gathered.

Therefore, depending upon the context, Sheol can mean the grave, the unseen realm of the dead, as well as the special place where the wicked reside.

Sheol is also used symbolically in a number of contexts. It is used as the place from where the righteous are saved. Sheol can also refer to a combination of these symbolic meanings.

The context must always determine the meaning. "Grave" is probably the best English word to translate Sheol in most contexts. Sheol is often described as being a dark lonely realm under the earth.

In the Old Testament, there seems to be no distinction between the righteous and the unrighteous in Sheol. This distinction between the believers and unbelievers is made clear in the New Testament.

Sheol, or the grave, will continue until the resurrection of the dead. Since Sheol is a temporary in-between state for the deceased, it will come to an end someday. Like death itself, Sheol will be cast into the lake of fire never to exist again.

How Is Sheol
Described?

Sheol, the grave, or possibly the place where the spirits of the dead congregate, is described in a number of ways in the Old Testament. The following descriptions are given of Sheol.

1. SHEOL HAS GATES OR BARS

Sheol is symbolically described as having gates or bars. In the Book of Job, we read the following about Sheol.

> *Will* they go down to the gates of Sheol? Shall *we have* rest together in the dust? (Job 17:16 NKJV).

While the New King James translations uses the word "gates" it has been also translated as "bars." The New Revised Standard Bible says.

> Will it go down to the bars of Sheol? Shall we descend together into the dust? (Job 17:16 NRSV).

The idea seems to be that people cannot escape from its presence. Therefore, the place has gates or bars to keep the residents inside.

2. IT IS DARK AND GLOOMY

Sheol is a place that is dark and gloomy. In the Book of Job, it also says.

If I look for Sheol as my house, if I spread my couch in darkness (Job 17:13 NRSV).

This is certainly an ominous description of death and the grave.

3. THERE IS SORROW IN SHEOL

There is sorrow in Sheol, the place of death. We read in Samuel.

The sorrows of Sheol surrounded me; the snares of death confronted me (2 Samuel 22:6 NKJV).

Sheol is a place of sorrow.

4. THERE IS PAIN IN SHEOL

Sheol is also described as a place of pain. The psalmist wrote of the pangs or pain of Sheol He put it in this manner.

The snares of death encompassed me; the pangs of Sheol laid hold on me; I suffered distress and anguish (Psalm 116:3 ESV).

There is distress and anguish in Sheol.

5. SHEOL IS A PLACE OF DARKNESS AND SILENCE

Sheol is a lowly region of darkness and silence. In the Book of Job, it describes it in this way.

The land of gloom like thick darkness, like deep shadow without any order, where light is as thick darkness (Job 10:22 ESV).

There is both darkness and silence in this region.

6. IT IS A PLACE OF SHADOWS

Sheol is a place where people are mere shadows of their former selves. Isaiah described them in the following manner.

Sheol from beneath is excited over you to meet you when you come; It arouses for you the spirits of the dead, all the leaders of the earth; It raises all the kings of the nations from their thrones. They will all respond and say to you, 'Even you have been made weak as we, you have become like us' (Isaiah 14:9,10 NRSV).

It is also the place of shadows, a place of weakness, not of strength.

Thus, we find that Sheol is described to us in a number of graphic ways in the Bible.

The fact that the realm of the dead is described in this manner further illustrates the need for an authoritative word concerning what happens to the dead. To take away the terror of the unknown, we need to know what to expect.

The good news is that God's Word, the Bible, gives us authoritative answers. We do not have to be ignorant about the afterlife!

SUMMARY TO APPENDIX 2
HOW IS SHEOL DESCRIBED?

Sheol, which represents death, the grave, and perhaps in certain contexts the unseen realm of the dead, is described in a number of ways in Scripture. Often these descriptions are from the perspective of those which are still living. These symbolic representations include a place that has gates, somewhere where it is dark and gloomy, a place of sorrow, a place of pain, a place of darkness and silence, and a place where the wicked are a shadow of their former selves.

These graphic descriptions make the point that death is still an enemy. The grave holds terror for the living because it is the great unknown. Sheol, when used in many Old Testament contexts, reflects this fear of the next world as far as the living are concerned.

This again illustrates the need for God's divine revelation on the subject so that we can know exactly what lies ahead for those who have passed on to the next world. Indeed, for without divine revelation, the grave holds nothing but fear and dread.

APPENDIX 3

Who Are The Shades Which Live In Sheol? (The Rephaim)

In a few places in the Old Testament there are personages spoken of as existing in Sheol, or in the underworld, called, "shades." Who are these shades? What do we know about them?

THE SHADES (REPHAIM)

The English word "shade" is a translation of the Hebrew word *rephaim*. Interestingly, this Hebrew word has a double usage in the Old Testament. On the one hand, it describes an ancient people called the Rephaites. They were also known as giants. For example, we read of them in Deuteronomy.

> Like the Anakites, they too were considered Rephaites, but the Moabites called them Emites (Deuteronomy 2:11 NIV).

The New King James Version translates the word as "giants." It says.

> They were also regarded as giants, like the Anakim, but the Moabites call them Emim (Deuteronomy 2:11 NKJV).

The word "rephaim" is also used of an actual place. It says in Samuel.

> Once again the Philistines came up, and were spread out in the valley of Rephaim (2 Samuel 5:22 NRSV).

While this word can refer to this particular group of people who lived here on the earth, as well a geographical place, there are a few times in the Old Testament where this word specifically refers to the realm of the dead or shadowy individuals living in this dark realm. These references are found in the books of Job, Psalms, Proverbs, and Isaiah.

WHY DOES THE SAME WORD REFER TO GIANTS AS WELL AS THE DEAD?

It has puzzled many Bible students as to why the same word would refer to a race of giants and then to those shadowy figures in the realm of the dead. A number of possible solutions have been suggested.

Perhaps the best solution is to see it as a contrast between the powerful living and the weak dead. The rephaim were the great people of ancient society. Indeed, they were kings and warriors.

However, when these great men entered the realm of the dead they were as weak as the weakest common person. In other words, those who were the powerful and mighty in this life did not bring their power with them to the next life. In other words, they were like everyone else. If this is the correct understanding of the double usage of this term, then it teaches us a powerful lesson.

The following are a list of references to the dead as "shades." From these few places we can learn some important truths about them.

THE SHADES LIVE BELOW

In the Book of Job we read the following about the shades.

> The shades below tremble, the waters and their inhabitants (Job 26:5 NRSV).

The translation, God's Word, puts it this way.

> The souls of the dead tremble beneath the water, and so do the creatures living there (Job 26:5 God's Word).

In this passage, the shades are said to be existing somewhere "below the water."

THE SHADES ARE EQUATED WITH THE DEAD

In Psalms, we find the shades equated with the dead. The psalmist wrote.

> Do you work wonders for the dead? Do the shades rise up to praise you? Selah (Psalm 88:5 NRSV).

The New International Version translates it in this manner.

> Do you show your wonders to the dead? Do those who are dead rise up and praise you? Selah (Psalm 88:5 NIV).

Here the shades are the dead.

THE SHADES ARE EQUATED WITH DEATH

The next time this rare word is used is in the Book of Proverbs. It says.

> For her way leads down to death, and her paths to the shades (Proverbs 2:18 NRSV).

The Holman Christian Standard Bible translates it in this manner.

> For her house sinks down to death and her ways to the land of the departed spirits (Proverbs 2:18 HCSB).

The land of the shades is the land of departed spirits.

THE SHADES ARE THE DEAD

In another instance in Proverbs, the shades refer to the dead. It states the following.

> But they do not know that the dead are there, that her guests are in the depths of Sheol (Proverbs 9:18 NRSV).

The word translated "dead" is the Hebrew word "rephaim." Here it indicates the shades of Sheol, those who live in shadows.

THE SHADES ARE THE ASSEMBLY OF THE DEAD

Again, we find the word used in Proverbs. In this case, most English translations translate the word as "assembly of the dead" rather than shades. For example, the New Revised Standard Version translates the verse in this manner.

> Whoever wanders from the way of understanding will rest in the assembly of the dead (Proverbs 21:16 NRSV).

The shades are equated with the assembly of the dead.

THE SHADES GREET THOSE WHO COME TO SHEOL

In the Book of Isaiah, we read again of these shades. It says that they are the ones who greet those who come to Sheol, to the realm of the dead.

> Sheol beneath is stirred up to meet you when you come; it rouses the shades to greet you, all who were leaders of the earth; it raises from their thrones all who were kings of the nations (Isaiah 14:9 NRSV).

The Holman Christian Standard Bible puts it this way.

> Sheol below is eager to greet your coming. He stirs up the spirits of the departed for you—all the rulers of the earth. He makes all the kings of the nations rise from their thrones (Isaiah 14:9 HCSB).

These dead spirits are eager to greet those who arrive.

THE SHADES REMAIN DEAD

In another instance in Isaiah we read about how the shades are not able to rise up and come back to live on the earth. We read.

The dead do not live; shades do not rise-because you have punished and destroyed them, and wiped out all memory of them (Isaiah 26:14 NRSV).

The translation God's Word puts it this way.

The wicked are dead. They are no longer alive. The spirits of the dead won't rise. You have punished them, destroyed them, and wiped out all memory of them (Isaiah 26:14 God's Word).

Here they are the called "the spirits of the dead." These spirits will not rise back to life on this earth. Indeed, the next time they will arise will be on judgment day when they are sent away to eternal punishment.

THE GREAT OLD TESTAMENT PASSAGE ON THE RESURRECTION

The final reference to the shades is also found in Isaiah. Here the word is again referring to the "dead." This passage is one of the greatest Old Testament passages referring to the future resurrection of the dead. It reads.

Your dead will live. Their corpses will rise. Those who lie dead in the dust will wake up and shout for joy, because your dew is a refreshing dew, and the earth will revive the spirits of the dead (Isaiah 26:19 God's Word).

The dead will someday live. The shades will be revived by the Lord Himself. This wonderful promise of the resurrection of the dead is further developed in the New Testament.

This summarizes the references to these shadowy individuals who live in the realm of the dead, the shades.

SUMMARY TO APPENDIX 3
WHO ARE THE SHADES WHICH LIVE IN SHEOL? (THE REPHAIM)

On a few occasions, the Old Testament refers to those living in Sheol as "shades." They are describes as spirits of the dead who are merely a shadow of their former selves. They exist in the realm of the dead and they remain dead. Indeed, they cannot come back to life.

It is difficult to develop any real doctrine about these shades because the few texts in which they are referred to are not historical texts but rather poetical. In other words, we are not given specific facts about these shades since we read about them in non-historical contexts.

What makes matters more difficult is that the same Hebrew word, *rephaim*, is used of an ancient race of people who were characterized as giants, powerful men in the ancient world.

The best solution to this problem seems to lie in the contrast between the powerful living rephaim and the dead weak shades. These dominant individuals of the ancient world were as weak as the weakest common person when they reached the realm of the dead. Their riches, power and might were not brought over with them in the afterlife. They were like everyone else in the next world.

This is consistent with what the remainder of the Scripture teaches about life and death. We enter the world with nothing and we leave the world with nothing. No matter how rich or powerful we may be, we do cannot take anything with us. Therefore, these powerful rulers, mighty men of the earth, became weak shadows of their former selves.

If this is the correct understanding of the two terms, sheol and rephaim then it teaches us a powerful lesson. Death is the great equalizer. Once an individual is dead, their riches, glory, and strength are all lost.

Consequently, humans need to prepare in this life for the things which really matter in the next life. This is one of the lessons we learn from the "shades."

About The Author

Don Stewart is a graduate of Biola University and Talbot Theological Seminary (with the highest honors).

Don is a best-selling and award-winning author having authored, or co-authored, over seventy books. This includes the best-selling *Answers to Tough Questions*, with Josh McDowell, as well as the award-winning book *Family Handbook of Christian Knowledge: The Bible*. His various writings have been translated into over thirty different languages and have sold over a million copies.

Don has traveled around the world proclaiming and defending the historic Christian faith. He has also taught both Hebrew and Greek at the undergraduate level and Greek at the graduate level.

OUR NEXT BOOK IN THE AFTERLIFE SERIES:
VOLUME 3

Resurrection And Judgment

As we have seen, the present state of the dead is only temporary. Indeed, there will come a day when the dead will be raised and judged. Our next book in the series on the afterlife will deal with questions concerning the resurrection of the dead and final judgments. In this book, we will answer questions such as these:

Why Do Believers Need A Resurrected Body?

What Will The Resurrected Bodies Of The Righteous Be Like?

On What Basis Will People Be Judged?

What Is The Last Judgment (The Great White Throne)

What Will Be The Results Of God's Final Judgment?

Made in the USA
San Bernardino, CA
25 July 2017